A Book of Prayers for Every Season

Digital Prayers and Promises Answered

Tisha Lynton Rose

Knowledge Power Books

ISBN: 978-09993455-8-0

Library of Congress Control Number: 2017959963

Cover Design and Editing: Knowledge Power Communication, Inc.

Published by

Knowledge Power Books
Valencia, CA 91355
www.knowledgepowerbooks.com

Printed in the United States of America

Dedication

This book is dedicated to my mom, Joan Wallace Lynton. She prayed for me. Now, I am honored to pray for her.

Introduction

The effectual, fervent prayers of the righteous avails much.

Why has it taken so long to write my first book? Everything is in the right time and season. I believe in prayer and the power of prayer. This book is birthed from my electronic intercession for others. When asked to pray or when I see a need for prayer, I text, tweet, post or email on the spot. This ensures that the need is covered in the event life gets hectic.

Over my years on Facebook, I have posted many prayers and a member of the church in which I serve, on multiple occasions, said to write a book. She said she would just print them to pray. One push to publish many of these prayers came when I saw one prayer I posted on another person's page. Hmm. Now, if that is not motivation.

You will notice the prayers date back to 2010, because I wanted you to see where I started. God answered these prayers and is still answering as I continue to pray and write. It doesn't matter where you start reading and using the prayers in the book, the dates aren't relative. I believe these prayers will impact your life tremendously. They will be the answer to a need at a particular time. You will see your life and situation through them. Just as this book is a seed of my faith, I encourage you to step out and move in your dreams and desires.

There may be times when situations may not be ideal, but we must move anyway. I recently had a very encouraging session with an author, speaker, and powerful example of where I want to go. That lit a fire under me and ignited this JUMP.

I thank God for His faithfulness. May one, two, three or more of these prayers encourage you as you read and believe.

– Tisha Lynton Rose

2010

Posted on Facebook March 18, 2010

Thanking God for allowing me to see another year of life as it is just past midnight, officially March 19th even though my dad always reminds me I was born 11:30 am or something like that. God promises to satisfy me with long, abundant life and show me His salvation and He is faithful.

Posted on Facebook April 15, 2010

It is because of the Lord's mercies that we are not consumed. Great is His faithfulness! My dad celebrates 70 blessed years tomorrow. God is so good! Thank you, Jesus!

Posted on Facebook April 30, 2010

Dear Heavenly Father, I pray for the Men of Valor and Excellence that they would have a blessed time of fun and fellowship, worship and wad cord. Lord, pour out and overflow in their lives individually and collectively. Saturate them with your presence. Thank you for traveling mercies and returning them changed with a hunger and thirst for more of you. Thank you for answered prayer. In the mighty, powerful name of Jesus! Amen!

Posted on Facebook July 31, 2010

This is THE DAY the Lord has made. I rejoice, and I am glad in it. Thank you, Lord for your faithfulness to me. I praise you for the husband you chose for me in Robert Rose before the foundation of the world. Thank you for two wonderful daughters in Jennifer and Maya. Thank you for family and friends!

Posted on Facebook October 6, 2010

Dear Lord, thank you for another chance to say thank you! I am grateful for your grace and mercy, your love and forgiveness. I declare that this day is peace-filled, favor-filled, productive, and directed by you. Thank you for your protection over my family and friends. In Jesus' name, so be it.

Posted on Facebook October 7, 2010

Good morning, Lord, thank you for watching over us through the night and allowing us to see this day. Nothing will catch you by surprise, so we will be led and directed by you. You promise never to leave us. Our confidence is in you. We love you, Lord. May everyone reading this be blessed today. In Jesus' name. Amen!

Posted on Facebook October 8, 2010

Dear Heavenly Father, thank you for another day. Thank you for your Son Jesus the way, the truth, and the life who gives us access to you God. I love you, Lord. I praise you with the breath you gave me. I declare that this day cooperates with your plans for me. Father, please bless my family and FB friends. In Jesus' name, Amen!

Posted on Facebook October 29, 2010

Dear God, thank you for this morning rise, wonderful rest and protection as we slept. I love and adore you, Lord. Thank you for peace. Father, I lift up my family and friends and everyone reading this. I pray that you would bless, encourage, build up, heal, protect, save, strengthen and restore them. Be glorified in the lives of your people. Thank you, God! In Jesus' powerful and matchless name I pray, Amen. Have a great day!

Posted on Facebook November 8, 2010

Dear Lord, thank you for this new day. Father God I love and adore you. I pray for your guidance in everything I do and say. Holy Spirit, govern my thoughts. Lord, I pray that everyone reading this would have a blessed day. I pray for salvation for those who don't know You! Encourage hearts and minds. Heal bodies and restore relationships! I lift up my Pastors and LPCC family and thank you for the harvest. In Jesus' name. Amen.

Posted on Facebook November 18, 2010

Dear Heavenly Father, thank you for another day of life. Thank you, Lord, for your faithfulness. Thank you for opportunities to be used by You. I pray that You would bless our day and that it would be peaceful, productive and filled with favor. I pray for salvation of the unsaved and healing for every sick body. Jesus' blood was shed for our salvation and His body broken for our healing. I love You, Lord! Thank you, God! In Jesus' name. Amen.

Posted on Facebook November 28, 2010

Today, I Begin Again! I am inspired! I can do all things through Christ who strengthens me! I shall live and declare the works of the Lord! Dear Lord, give me a plan and the strength and determination to finish strong. Please provide the natural support I need. I have the will to win and live a healthy and whole life – spiritually, physical, financially, mentally and emotionally! Makeover Time! Thank you, Lord!

Posted on Facebook Thursday, December 2, 2010, 8:00 am

Dear Lord, thank you for another day! Guide me today and help me to manage all that needs to be accomplished. I declare it will be productive, favor-filled and peace-filled. Thank you, Father! In Jesus' name, so be it! Have a great day FB friends! Let's make a difference!

2011

Posted on Facebook January 11, 2011

Praying for my family right now on the death of my grandmother's sister. Dear Lord, comfort everyone right now and surround us with your peace. Be with her husband, children, and grandchildren as they make the necessary preparations. Facilitate finances and travel for everyone desiring to fellowship with the family. Thank you, Lord, for the opportunity to speak with her at the end of last year! In Jesus' name! Amen!!!

Posted on Facebook January 12, 2011

Dear God, thank for another day to make a difference. Use me for your glory. Father, I pray that every FB friend would have a good day. I thank you for breakthrough in our lives! You are worthy of all praise, honor and glory! You are faithful to watch over Your word to perform it. Thank you, Father! In Jesus' name. Amen!

Posted on Facebook January 19, 2011

Dear Lord, nothing is hidden from You. I pray that the suspect is found without further delay. I pray for peace and calm for EVERYONE involved and affected by this incident. I come against fear and frustration in the name of Jesus and plead the blood of Jesus over the injured officer that all will be well. In Jesus' name, I pray. Amen!

Posted on Facebook January 20, 2011

This is the day the Lord has made. I rejoice and am glad in it. Dear God, I pray for peace to saturate all Southern California especially our schools. I pray for order and calm so that it would be a productive day for all. Lord, we welcome your presence in our schools. You're the only solution/savior. Thank you, Father for your grace and mercy. In Jesus' name, amen. Have a great day FB friends!

Posted on Facebook January 29, 2011

Dear Lord, thank you for two wonderful parents! I celebrate today, January 30th, their 43rd anniversary. Thank you for satisfying them with long, abundant, healthy life and showing them your salvation. Their later shall be greater than their past. Bless them today with much love, joy, and peace! In Jesus' name, I pray, Amen!

Posted on Facebook February 3, 2011

Anticipate the best! Expect the great! Thank you, Lord, for this reminder. All things are possible with You. I can do all things through Christ who strengthens me. Dear Heavenly Father, guide and direct me in everything I do, say and think. Bless, heal, strengthen, encourage, protect and comfort my FB friends where they need it today. Thank you, Lord, for your love, mercy and grace. In Jesus' name, Amen! Make it a great day!

Posted on Facebook February 17, 2011

Dear Lord, please give me the energy, confidence, strength, stamina, health to make it through this work out. In Jesus' mighty and powerful name! Amen

Posted on Facebook February 22, 2011

Dear Lord, thank you for health, strength, energy and endurance to conquer this workout. In Jesus' name, I pray. Amen!

Posted on Facebook February 24, 2011

Dear Lord, I can do all things through your strength. I need strength to do this workout. I also pray the trainer is having a great day. Thank you, Father!

Posted on Facebook February 26, 2011

Father God, You are mighty. I pray You arise and demonstrate Your power on behalf of my FB friends. Show Yourself strong this day on their behalf. Thank you, Lord!

Posted on Facebook March 14, 2011

Dear Lord, thank you for another day! Father, use me for your glory. I declare this day is peace-filled, productive, favor-filled and everything/everyone cooperates with the plans You God have purposed for me before. FBF, have a dynamic day!

Posted on Facebook March 14, 2011

Father God, I lift up every lady in the Woven Winners Circle. They can do everything they need to do in life through Christ. You love them unconditionally. Overflow in their life to meet their every need. Thank you, Lord! In Jesus' name. Amen!

Posted on Facebook March 31, 2011

Father God I thank you for seeing me through this month. You continue to be faithful! I thank you for the victory! I am blessed! Thanks again to everyone who stopped by to show some birthday love. I was determined to thank everyone personally as you took the time to share with me. I pray that everyone have a wonderful weekend!

Posted on Facebook April 5, 2011

Dear Lord, thank you for traveling mercies for all who have made it to FL so far. I pray for safe, timely travel for everyone who will be coming to HCASC this year. Thank you for a productive week of preparation without stress and frustration. Work everything out for our good and Your glory. Lord, bless my family and friends. In Jesus' name, Amen!

Posted on Facebook April 7, 2011

Dear Lord, thank you for last night's rest and this morning's rise. I pray that it will be a peace-filled and productive, fruitful and favor-filled day! Bless my family and FB friends. Father God, you are faithful! I love You and thank You, Lord! Use me for your glory. In Jesus' mighty and powerful name, I pray! Amen! Have a great day all!

Posted on Facebook April 7, 2011

Dear Heavenly Father, thank you for this very productive day! Please multiply my sleep 7 hours to the hour, that I may wake rested and refreshed. Please give sweet sleep and supernatural strength to Robert and may his Friday be productive. In Jesus' mighty and powerful name, I pray and with thanksgiving! Amen!

Posted on Facebook April 8, 2011

Dear Lord, I thank you that this day is already productive and favor-filled. May everything be for our good and your glory! I pray for traveling mercies for everyone making their way to HCASC22. Order my steps and my speech. Bless and protect my family and FB friends. In Jesus' name, I pray, Amen! Make it a great day FB friends! Speak Life!

Posted on Facebook April 8, 2011

Thank you, God, for a good day today! Dear Lord, as I close my eyes, I pray for sweet sleep. As I lay down to rest may I wake refreshed. Lord, I pray for traveling grace for every team, president and guest making their way to HCASC22 by bus, car or plane that they would all arrive without accident or incident. Thank you, Father! In Jesus' name, Amen!

Posted on Facebook April 9, 2011

Dear God, thank you for a super productive day with everyone due into HCASC 22 today arriving safely. Lord, I need sweet sleep tonight and supernatural strength as I wake shortly. Please multiply these 4+ hours to feel more like 10. God, you are faithful, and I am grateful. In Jesus' name, Amen!

Posted on Facebook April 11, 2011

Dear Lord, I pray for sweet sleep tonight and safe travels for everyone returning home throughout the day tomorrow. Thank you, Father! I am grateful!

Posted on Facebook April 26, 2011

Dear Lord, thank you for another day. I pray its peace-filled, productive and favor-filled. I plead the blood of Jesus over my body. I pray for everyone attending WWW this week that they would have a supernatural encounter with you. Bless their family. Bless Dr. B and New Light church. Bless Pastor Linda and use her for your glory! Thank you, Father! You are faithful! I love you, Lord! In Jesus' name! Have a great day all!

Posted on Facebook April 30, 2011

Dear Lord, the last two months of my life did not take you by surprise. I need your direction and strength. Please order my steps, literally, especially today. Thank you, God, for Your continued faithfulness! In Jesus' name, I pray. Amen. Happy day all!

Posted on Facebook May 13, 2011

Dear Lord, I pray for a full recovery and complete healing for Bryan Stow. Please strengthen and encourage his family and friends. I pray that You would reveal and bring to justice the ones involved in this attack. Thank you, Father. In Jesus' name.

Posted on Facebook May 15, 2011

Dear Lord, as I watch the news regarding Bryan's transport on Monday morning, I pray that Your presence will facilitate every detail from the hospital in LA to the jet to the medical facility in San Francisco. God move in a mighty way for a supernatural recovery. In Jesus' name, amen!

Posted on Facebook May 18, 2011

Dear Heavenly Father, this is the day that you have made. I rejoice and am glad in it! Thank you for soundness of mind, breath in my body and the ability to move. God, You are faithful. Thank you for brand new mercy. Order my steps and my actions. I pray for favor concerning 10237-C. I pray this would be a productive, peace-filled day. I lift up my family and FB friends. Thank you, Lord! In Jesus' matchless name. Amen!

Posted on Facebook May 19, 2011

Dear Heavenly Father, I lift up my family and FB friends and pray for spiritual, physical, mental, emotional, financial and relationship healing and restoration in their lives with themselves, with You God and with others. Heal all hurt Lord. Demonstrate Your power this day. In Jesus' name, I pray with thanksgiving. Amen. Have a great day!

Posted on Facebook May 20, 2011

Dear God, You've given us another day and we thank You. You are faithful and can be trusted. We praise You and give You all honor and glory! In Jesus' name, Amen. Have a fantastic, favor-filled Friday FB friends! Remember, Jesus loves you!

Posted on Facebook May 21, 2011

Thank you, Lord, for this beautiful day! Thank you for strength in my body, soundness of mind and my soul secured in you! Thank you for family, friends and fellowship! Father God, thank you for your continued faithfulness! I love You, Lord, and give You all honor and glory! In Jesus' mighty and matchless name I pray, Amen!

Posted on Facebook May 26, 2011

Dear Heavenly Father, I need Your Super added to my natural for mental and physical strength, energy and endurance for today's workout. Thank you, Lord You know! In Jesus' mighty name. Amen.

Posted on Facebook May 30, 2011

Dear Heavenly Father, I lift up my family and FB friends to You right now and pray that You would minister peace to them. I pray for those already sleeping, those preparing to sleep and those who can't. Heal the sick, comfort the bereaved, and save the lost. Thank you, Lord. You're a very present help. In Jesus' mighty name I pray, amen. God is faithful and can be trusted.

Posted on Facebook June 1, 2011

Dear Heavenly Father, thank you for this new day of life. I love, honor and adore You. I thank you for mercy and grace. Forgive me of my sins in word, thought or deed. Create in me a clean heart and renew a right spirit in me. Thank you, Father, for never leaving me or forsaking me. Thank you for Your love and compassion even in times of correction. Speak to me and through me and use me for your glory. Have your way in my life...

Posted on Facebook June 1, 2011

As we pray this day touching in agreement for this land, I plead the blood of Jesus over our families. Father, I lift up President Obama and our national and local governments and pray that godly wisdom would reign. I pray for revival in the land. I pray for repentance and turning away from our wicked ways. I pray for humility and are turn to you Lord God. You promise to hear from heaven, forgive our sins and heal our land...

Posted on Facebook June 1, 2011

Father God, I thank you for breath in my body. I thank you for the want to and ability to walk. I bind my mind to the mind of Christ and see myself as You see me. Thank you for the shed blood of Jesus for my salvation and his broken body for my healing. Do a new thing in me, Lord. I lift up my family, FB friends and their family and pray that You would minister to them right now. Thank you for freedom to pray and praise. In Jesus' name.

Posted on Facebook June 13, 2011

Dear Heavenly Father, thank you for another day and work week. I lift up my family and FB friends and pray that you bless them with peace and protection, comfort and healing, strength and breakthrough. I pray for those in need of salvation. Lord, please move like only You can. Thank you! In Jesus' name, Amen. Have a productive day filled with favor FB friends!

Posted on Facebook June 15, 2011

Father God, set a guard over my mouth and keep me in perfect peace that my actions and attitude may bring You glory. May the words I speak be seasoned with love and bring wisdom to the hearers. I come against distractions and frustration in the name of Jesus and speak peace to my environment. Thank you, Lord!

Posted on Facebook June 19, 2011

Dear Heavenly Father, thank you for Your grace and mercy and Your loving correction. I thank you for never leaving or forsaking me or giving up on me. Forgive me of my sins and help me to be who You've called me to be in every area of life. Bless fathers everywhere and heal relationships today. Thank you, Lord! I love You and honor You, Lord! In Jesus' name, I pray, Amen! Have a blessed day FB friends!

Posted on Facebook June 21, 2011

Dear Heavenly Father, thank you for this day of new grace and mercy. Please order my steps, guide my attitude and actions and orchestrate my day! Please bless, strengthen, heal, comfort and protect my family and FB friends! I declare peace, productivity and favor over my day! Thank you, God, for Your faithfulness! In Jesus' mighty name I pray, Amen. FB friends have a great God-ordained day! Stay hydrated.

Posted on Facebook June 22, 2011

I can do everything I need to do today through Christ! Dear God, thank you for wisdom and insight, motivation and inspiration for today's assignment. Cover my mind and guard my heart. Use me for Your glory. Thank you, Lord! In Jesus' mighty name. Amen. Hallelujah!

Posted on Facebook June 24, 2011

Dear Heavenly Father, thank you for this new day! I declare that everything and everyone will cooperate with the plans, You have for me. Order my steps, direct my actions and my attitude. Guide me Holy Spirit. I pray for peace, favor and productivity. May the girls have a fun, safe day on this last day of school. I pray for protection and plead the blood of Jesus over them. Thank you, Lord! In Jesus' name, Amen. Be blessed FBF!

Posted on Facebook June 26, 2011

Thank you, Father for this wonderful day of worship, word, walking, washing clothes and everything in between. It's been y camp tomorrow, I pray a hedge of protection over them and Your presence to guide them. Thank you, God! In Jesus' name. Amen.

Posted on Facebook June 29, 2011

Thank you, Lord, for this productive day! Thank you for the first six months of 2011. Please rest me tonight that I may wake refreshed. I pray for Your presence and protection, wisdom and favor tomorrow. Be glorified in my life. Thank you for Your grace and mercy. Please forgive me of my sins. Bless my family and FB friends. In Jesus' name, Amen. Goodnight!

Posted on Facebook July 5, 2011

Dear Heavenly Father, I lift up my family and FB friends and pray for comfort for the bereaved, strength for the weak and weary, healing for the sick, encouragement for the discouraged and depressed, joy for those mourning, breakthrough for those on the brink, favor for the faithful, salvation for the spiritually lost and rededication for those who walked away from You! Thank you, Lord! In Jesus' name, Amen! Be blessed!

Posted on Facebook July 5, 2011

Father God, thank you for this wonderful day! I lift up the families who have lost loved ones in the past few days. Please comfort and strengthen them. Love on them and encourage them with Your peace! Lord, move in the lives of Your people like only You can. Thank you, Heavenly Father! In Jesus' name, amen! Good night FB!

Posted on Facebook July 8, 2011

Dear Heavenly Father, thank you for this new day to serve You in everything I do and say. May my attitude and actions be pleasing to You.

Use me for Your glory. Forgive my sins and quicken me, Holy Spirit, to immediately repent when I mess up. Set a guard over my mouth and a hedge around my mind. Cover my heart Lord! I love You and adore You. Help me to love like You do. Order my steps and direct my path. Thank you, Lord!

Posted on Facebook July 13, 2011

Dear Heavenly Father, thank you for another day. Thank you for breath in my body. Thank you for a sound mind that I bind to the mind of Christ. Thank you for protection. Thank you for family. Thank you for grace and mercy. Thank you for love and forgiveness. Thank you for the shed blood and broken body of Your Son. Thank you for eternal life through Him. Thank you for Your faithfulness. Thank you for and bless each FB friend. In Jesus' name, Amen.

Posted on Facebook July 18, 2011

Dear Lord, I lift up my Pastors, Dr. Fred Hodge and Pastor Linda Hodge and pray that You would refresh them and restore everything they gave out in ministering to Your people on Sunday. Father, move in a mighty way in their lives this day, this week. Thank you, Lord! In Jesus' name, Amen.

Posted on Facebook July 18, 2011

Dear Heavenly Father, thank You for this new day. Help me to see things through Your eyes so that I can handle situations with wisdom and understanding. Remind me to think before I speak and pray before I act. May Your will be done through me today. Bless my family and FB friends. In Jesus' name, I pray. Amen. Have a great day all!

Posted on Facebook July 18, 2011

Dear Lord, I lift up everyone preparing for and serving/ministering at the WOVEN conference this week. I plead the blood of Jesus over them, their health, family, finances and work schedules. I come against all distractions. Strengthen everyone for this assignment. Thank you, Lord, In Jesus' name. Amen.

Posted on Facebook July 20, 2011

Dear Heavenly Father, thank you for this new day. I lift up my family and FB friends and pray for shelter and provision for the homeless, employment for the unemployed, healing for the sick, comfort for the bereaved, salvation for the lost. Lord, be their joy, strength, peace. Thank you, Lord, for Your faithfulness! In Jesus' name, Amen. Have a productive, peace-filled day all!

Posted on Facebook July 22, 2011

Dear Heavenly Father, thank you for a new day of grace and mercy. Thank you for protection and provision. Thank you for peace and a sound mind. Thank you for health and wholeness. Thank you for salvation for loved ones. Thank you for favor. Thank you for makeover and breakthrough. Thank you, just because You are God! I love you, Lord! In Jesus' mighty name I pray, Amen! Have a blessed, favor-filled Friday family and FB friends!

Posted on Facebook July 23, 2011

Dear Lord, please rest and refresh everyone who ministered, served, attended and are yet serving to wrap up and put things back in order. May their sleep be multiplied 7 hours to the hour. May there be no backlash and may every seed of time, talent and treasure reap a supernatural return. In Jesus' name, thank you, Father. Amen.

Posted on Facebook July 23, 2011

To Rest In Peace in death, we must receive and serve Christ in life. Dear Heavenly Father, I lift up my FB friends experiencing bereavement and grief right now and pray that you would comfort them and their family members. Heal their hurt and pain. I pray for strength, unity and peace. Thank you, Lord! In Jesus' name, Amen!

Posted on Facebook July 26, 2011

Dear Heavenly Father, thank you for a new day! Thank you for grace and mercy. I pray for and thank you in advance for comfort for the bereaved, healing for the physically challenged, encouragement for the discouraged, peace for the confused, salvation for the lost, joy for all. You are faithful and can be trusted! You are worthy to be praised! I love and adore You! In Jesus' name. Amen. Have a blessed day family and FB friends!

Posted on Facebook July 29, 2011

Dear Heavenly Father, I thank you for Your continued faithfulness! I lift up my family and FB friends and pray that they would have a favor-filled weekend of food, fellowship and fun. You know their needs so provide love, comfort, strength, healing, joy and salvation where needed. Meet the spiritual and financial needs. Demonstrate Your presence and power in the US government this weekend. Thank you, Lord! In Jesus' name, Amen.

Posted on Facebook August 4, 2011

Dear God, thank you for this day. You are faithful, and I trust you! Help me to make decisions pleasing to you. Guide my attitude and actions. Show up and show out where you know I need you right now. Use me for your glory. Thank you, Lord! In Jesus' mighty and powerful name, Amen! Have a blessed day family and FB friends!

Posted on Facebook August 4, 2011

Dear Heavenly Father, nothing catches You by surprise and the times are in Your hand. Father, I pray for protection and plead the blood of Jesus over the state of CA. I come against massive destruction and loss of life. Have mercy Lord. Only You know of the accuracy of these predictions. You have watched over us, so I will lay down to rest trusting You to keep us. In Jesus' mighty and powerful name. Amen.

Posted on Facebook August 7, 2011

Dear Heavenly Father, I lift up all our military and specifically the US "Navy Seals" Team6 and their families. Please comfort and strengthen anyone connected to those 31 team members who died in the helicopter crash. Surround them with Supernatural peace and heal their hurt. Protect our troops. Thank you, Lord! In Jesus' name, Amen.

Posted on Facebook August 7, 2011

Dear Heavenly Father, thank you for this life-changing, destiny-altering weekend. I see and feel the shift. I am in expectation of what is to come. Be glorified in and through my life. I believe for the manifestation! BAM! Thank you, Lord! In Jesus' name, Amen.

Posted on Facebook August 9, 2011

Dear Heavenly Father, please guide my attitude and actions and guard my heart and hearing. Thank you, Lord! In Jesus' name, amen! Have a blessed, productive, peace-filled, favor-filled day family and FB friends!

Posted on Facebook August 14, 2011

Dear God, thank you for this dynamic day of wonderful worship, powerful preaching, family fellowship, sisterly sharing and marriage ministry. Please bless my family, Pastors and church family. Use me for your glory. Have Your way. In Jesus' name I pray, Amen!

Posted on Facebook August 15, 2011

Dear Heavenly Father, I lift up the family of Pastor Zachery Tims. Please comfort and encourage his children Zoelle, Zachery III, Zahria and Zion and their mother as well as the New Destiny Christian Center family. Facilitate all arrangements that need to be made and minister Your peace to all involved. I pray for healing for all who have been touched and impacted in any way by his passing. Thank you, Lord! In Jesus' mighty name I pray, Amen!

Posted on Facebook August 17, 2011

Dear Heavenly Father, I lift up the body of Christ and pray for healing and restoration. I pray for a return to righteousness. I pray for broken relationships to be mended. Forgive me of my sins. Create in me a clean heart and renew a right spirit in me and use me as an agent of change for our good and your glory. Thank you Lord, for Your grace and mercy! God, You are faithful! In Jesus' mighty and matchless name I pray with thanksgiving, Amen! Have a blessed day family and FB friends. Make a difference today!

Posted on Facebook August 17, 2011

Dear Heavenly Father, thank you for stopping the enemy. I plead the blood of Jesus over all our schools and colleges and pray for protection this academic year. Thank you, Lord. In Jesus' name, amen!

Posted on Facebook August 18, 2011

Dear Heavenly Father, I lift up our HBCUs, the Presidents/Chancellors, Faculty, Staff and Students and pray for guidance for effective management and productivity. I pray for funding and favor. I pray for You to be invited to guide the direction for the future success of these institutions this year and beyond. Lord, thank you! In Jesus' name, Amen. Proud to be an HBCU grad!

Posted on Facebook August 19, 2011

Dear Heavenly Father, You are so, so on time. Thank you for ministering to me through this morning's Focus on the Family radio program. Speak to the girls about what they heard. Holy Spirit, help me to be the wife and mother God has called me to be. God, You are faithful! Thank you, Lord! In Jesus' mighty name I pray, Amen!

Posted on Facebook August 20, 2011

Dear Heavenly Father, help me to keep my attitudes and actions aligned with your Son Jesus that my witness for You will be effective. Thank you, Lord! In Jesus' name, Amen. Have a wonderful weekend family and FB friends!

Posted on Facebook August 22, 2011

Dear Heavenly Father, thank you for another day. Keep us focused on who we are and the authority we have. Order our steps. May our attitude and actions be pleasing to You. Surround and protect us. Use us to be a blessing. We declare peace and productivity over our day and command everyone (including us) and everything cooperate with Your plans for us. Thank you for Your faithfulness. We love and honor you. In Jesus' name, Amen!

Posted on Facebook August 22, 2011

Father God, I pray that You heal and save the baby dropped from the 3rd floor hospital structure in Orange County this evening. Reveal and direct the authorities to the person who did it. Thank you, Lord. In Jesus' name, Amen!

Posted on Facebook August 23, 2011

Dear Heavenly Father, thank you for this new day! There is no one like You and I am grateful for Your love, grace and mercy. Great is Your faithfulness. Please direct my day and order my steps. Use me for Your glory. May my attitude and actions be pleasing to You. Bless, heal, comfort, deliver and save my family and FB friends. Thank you, Lord! In Jesus' name, Amen. Have a dynamic, favor-filled day all!

Posted on Facebook August 24, 2011

Dear Heavenly Father, I thank you for favor in this real estate transaction. I come against delays and distractions. I call the condo sold NOW. Thank you, Lord. In Jesus' name, amen!

Posted on Facebook August 24, 2011

Countdown to first family vacay.... yeah! Dear Heavenly Father, thank you for Your faithfulness. I pray for favor w/everyone we come in contact with and for traveling mercies and protection. I pray that the fellowship with family would be good and enjoyable. Thank you for new life this week on the birth of my third niece. Bless everyone in that household. Lord, bless my family and FB friends! You know what they need. Thank you, Lord! In Jesus' name, amen! Have a wonderful week and weekend FB friends!

Posted on Facebook August 26, 2011

Dear Lord, thank you for the fun and fellowship with family today. Thank you for the praise reports. I lift up the prayer requests. Please forgive me of my sins and help me to be who You've called me to be. Use me for Your glory. Bless my family and FB friends. In Jesus' name. Amen.

Posted on Facebook August 29, 2011

Dear Heavenly Father, thank you for another day. Thank you for Your faithfulness throughout this trip. I pray for favor and protection to go before and with us as we return. Please bless our family and FB friends. Heal, comfort, strengthen, save and deliver where it's needed. You alone are worthy, and I give You the glory, honor and praise. Thank you, Lord! In Jesus' name, Amen. Have a dynamic day family and FB friends!

Posted on Facebook August 31, 2011

Father God, I lift up my family and plead the blood of Jesus over every member. I come against sickness, confusion and frustration, in the name of Jesus. I speak peace and order to the atmosphere and declare Your perfect will for us will be done. Arrest every contrary spirit. The devil was defeated and we give him no power to operate in our lives. We have the victory. Thank you, Lord. Demonstrate Your power right now. In Jesus' mighty, powerful, matchless name I pray with thanksgiving, amen!

Posted on Facebook September 2, 2011

Dear Heavenly Father, thank you for this new day of new grace and mercy. Thank you for new revelation and insight. Thank you for wisdom and direction. Thank you for provision and protection. Thank you for soundness of mind and physical health. Bless them today! In Jesus' mighty name, amen! Have a fantastic, favor-filled Friday family and FB friends! God is faithful!

Posted on Facebook September 3, 2011

Dear Heavenly Father, thank you for a new day w/new grace and mercy. Great is Your faithfulness! Order my steps and direct my day. May my attitudes and actions be pleasing to You. I lift up my family and FB friends and pray they would have a safe, peaceful, favor-filled, fruitful holiday weekend. Thank you, Lord, for Your love and compassion. I pray that You would hear from heaven, forgive our sins and heal our land. In Jesus' name.

Posted on Facebook September 5, 2011

Dear God! Thank you for this day and for family and friends! Thank you for dynamic Pastors ordained for such a time as this. Thank you for the opportunity to serve, minister and be a blessing. Use me for your glory! Guide my attitude and actions. Give me wisdom to be the woman, wife and mother You've called me to be. Thank you for increase and elevation in every area of my life. Bless my family and FB friends today. In Jesus' name.

Posted on Facebook September 6, 2011

This is the day the Lord has made. I will rejoice and be glad in it. Dear Heavenly Father, thank you for continued faithfulness. Thank you for waking me early this morning and for the blessing of corporate prayer. Order my steps and direct my day. Bless my family and FB friends with peace, love and joy. Bless them spiritually, mentally, emotionally, physically and financially. Thank you, Lord! In Jesus' name, Amen! Have a great day all!

Posted on Facebook September 7, 2011

Dear Heavenly Father, Thank you for this first day of school. I plead the blood of Jesus over the girls, their classmates and their entire schools this entire academic year. I pray they would have good success and excel in all their classes. I pray for their teachers and all who have responsibility to impart to them. Thank you, Lord! In Jesus' name. Amen. Now off to work I go.

Posted on Facebook September 9, 2011

This is the day the Lord has made. Rejoice! Dear God, thank you for a new day! Thank you for Your mighty hand. Thank you for mercy and favor in the courtroom for those being set-up by the enemy. Thank you for comfort and strength for those who has lost loved ones. Thank you for healing for those with challenges. Thank you for salvation for the lost. Thank you for peace, love and joy for all. In Jesus' name, Amen. Have a favor-filled Friday all!

Posted on Facebook September 10, 2011

Dear Heavenly Father, thank you for Your continued faithfulness. I lift up our nation and pray that You would protect from destruction at the hand of the enemy. I pray for healing of hearts and minds as we remember. Touch all hurt in a mighty way. Lord, be exalted. I praise and honor You. In Jesus' name. Amen. Have a blessed day family and FB friends!

Posted on Facebook September 12, 2011

Dear Heavenly Father, thank you for a new day and work week. I pray for order and organization. I pray for a productive, stress-free week. Father God, minister to my family and FB friends at their place of need for healing, comfort, strength, peace, salvation or a supernatural intervention in the courtroom. I believe You. Thank you, Lord! In Jesus' mighty name, Amen. Have a God-blessed day all!

Posted on Facebook September 12, 2011

Dear Heavenly Father, thank you for your grace, mercy, love and forgiveness. Thank you for protecting me throughout this super long day. Forgive me of my sins. I lift up my family and FB friends and pray that You would minister to their need and demonstrate Your power on their behalf. Thank you for the victory! Thank you for breakthrough! Thank you, Lord for your faithfulness! In Jesus' name. Amen.

Posted on Facebook September 18, 2011

Father God, I thank You for this beautiful new day that You have made. I thank You that I am fearfully and wonderfully made in Your image. I thank You that I have the mind of Christ. In you I live, move and have my being. Order my steps and orchestrate my day. Use me for Your glory. Bless my family, FB friends and pastors and church family this day. Thank you, Lord, for hearing and answering! In Jesus' mighty name, Amen.

Posted on Facebook September 18, 2011

I decree peace, power, productivity and prosperity over my life. I decree my days are fruitful and favor-filled. I decree I walk in overflow and increase in every area. I decree I walk in health and wholeness. I decree

I have a disciplined mind and determined spirit. I decree I am anointed and will accomplish all God has for me to do. I walk by faith and not by sight. I have the victory! Thank you, Lord!

Posted on Facebook September 20, 2011

Father God, bless every ministry worker who sowed their time, talent and treasure for Your kingdom. Restore and refresh them as they rest tonight and strengthen those who went straight to work tonight and who will work tomorrow. Thank you, Lord, for a powerful service with a dynamic word by Bishop I. V. Hilliard! In Jesus' name, Amen.

Posted on Facebook September 21, 2011

Dear Heavenly Father, this is the day that you have made and I am glad and rejoice in it. I declare and decree order, favor, peace and productivity over my day. I pray for energy and strength. Thank you, Lord. You are faithful. In Jesus' name, Amen. Have a blessed day family and FB friends! Trust God.

Posted on Facebook September 22, 2011

Father God, thank you for safe travels home. Thank you, for two power-packed nights of prayer, praise and preaching. Thank you for the lives, ministry and testimony of Bishop IV Hilliard and Pastor Dr. Bridget. Thank you for my Pastors, Dr. Fred and Pastor Linda Hodge. Thank you for every PMT worker who served in any capacity. Pour out Your blessings. Rest me tonight that I would be refreshed in the morning. In Jesus' name, Amen.

Posted on Facebook September 22, 2011

Father God, I give You glory for the progress in Bryan Stow's recovery. I pray for supernatural healing and that You satisfy him with a long, abundant life and show him your salvation. Strengthen and encourage his family and meet their emotional and financial needs. Thank you, Jehovah Rapha. In Jesus' name. Amen.

Posted on Facebook September 23, 2011

Dear God, I thank you for a new day and this life changing week. Thank you for the courage and determination to push. I lift up my family and FB friends and pray that You move in and through their situation. Heal, comfort, strengthen, save, pardon, pour out love where needed. Thank you, Lord. In Jesus' mighty name, Amen. Be blessed family and FB friends!

Posted on Facebook September 24, 2011

Dear Heavenly Father, thank you for this new day. You are worthy to be praised and we give You all glory and honor. Order our steps and ordain our day. May it be filled with fun, family fellowship. Guide our attitude, actions and decisions. Use us for your glory. Bless, save, heal, comfort, encourage and strengthen our family and FB friends. Thank you, Lord! In Jesus' mighty and matchless name I pray, Amen. Have a wonderful weekend!

Posted on Facebook September 27, 2011

Grateful for my Pastors and church family! Dear Heavenly Father, I lift up Dr. Fred and Pastor Linda Hodge and pray for increase and overflow in their lives, family and ministry. Use them in a mighty way in your kingdom. Bless them beyond what they think or imagine. Thank you, Lord, for hearing and answering! In Jesus' powerful name, let my LPCC family say amen.

Posted on Facebook September 28, 2011

Dear Heavenly Father, thank You for a new day for it is You who has made it. Thank You for grace and mercy and love and forgiveness. Order my steps. I honor and adore You. Bless my family and FB friends. Move in our workplaces whether that be in the home, kingdom ministry or a secular job. Demonstrate Your power. Thank You, Lord, for who You are. I give You the glory! Hallelujah! I praise You! In Jesus' name, amen. Be blessed!

Posted on Facebook October 1, 2011

Dear Heavenly Father, I pray for and thank you in advance for the finances and flexibility to pursue purpose and passion. In Jesus' name, amen.

Posted on Facebook October 2, 2011

This is the day the Lord has made and I am rejoicing in it! Father God, I bless your name this morning. Thank you for never leaving or forsaking us. We enter Your gates with thanksgiving and Your courts with praise. Speak to us through the worship and the Word. Heal, comfort, encourage and save today. Thank you, Lord! In Jesus' name, amen. Have a blessed day family and FB friends!

Posted on Facebook October 3, 2011

Father God, thank you for this new day, for your presence, for salvation and forgiveness, for insight and revelation to walk in your power and authority, for protection, for breakthrough, for increase, for overflow, for acceleration, for healing, for victory, for a sound mind, for the gift of the Holy Spirit. In Jesus' name, amen. Have a blessed, God-directed day family and FB friends!

Posted on Facebook October 4, 2011

"There is no room in your life for defeat!" Linda Hodge, Woman Under Construction ~ Father God, I thank you that I am more than a conqueror and can do all things through Christ who strengthens me. I thank you that You in me is greater than he who is in the world. I thank you that limitations are broken and I have the victory. Order my steps and use me for your glory. In Jesus' name, amen. Be blessed family and FB friends!

Posted on Facebook October 5, 2011

Dear Heavenly Father, I am grateful for another day. I lift up my family and FB friends and pray that You would move in their lives. Save souls. Heal hearts, minds and bodies. Restore relationships. Provide finances. Comfort, strengthen and encourage. Lord, You're faithful.

We trust You! Thank you for hearing and answering. In Jesus' name, amen. Have a safe, blessed day!

Posted on Facebook October 10, 2011

Father God, thank you for a new day, for health, strength, a sound mind and mobility. Thank you for Your saving grace, love, compassion, mercy, favor, protection, peace and constant presence. Thank you for shelter, provision and employment. Thank you for my family and friends. Thank you for my Pastors and church family. Use me for your glory today. In Jesus' name, amen! Have a blessed day family and FB friends!

Posted on Facebook October 10, 2011

Father God, I lift up everyone heading to Strategies NLC this week from Houston and out of town. Surround, protect them, shower them with favor and saturate them with Your presence. Pour out on Bishop I. V. and Dr. Bridget Hilliard and the entire New Light staff and ministry. Thank you, Lord, for this life-changing week of impact and impartation. Bless my Pastors and LPCC family in attendance. Thank you, Lord. In Jesus' name, amen.

Posted on Facebook October 11, 2011

Father God, Thank You for last night's rest and this morning's rise. This is the day You have made and I rejoice in it. Thank You for new mercies. Empower and equip me to be who you've called me to be. Order my steps and direct my day that You may get the glory. Thank you for my family. Thank you for my sisters in Christ. Thank you for a husband who loves You and me. You are faithful and I thank you. In Jesus' name, amen.

Posted on Facebook October 11, 2011

Father God, I pray for continued and complete recovery for Bryan Stow. Continue to strengthen and encourage his family. Meet their emotional and financial needs. Save souls and keep their minds in perfect peace. Thank you, Lord. In Jesus' name, amen.

Posted on Facebook October 11, 2011

Father God, I thank you for a new day. As I lay down to sleep, I thank you for love, peace and joy that only You can provide. I thank you for family and especially lift up to You my mom and brother-in-law as they each celebrate another year of life. Bless them and pour out on them just what they each need. God, You are faithful. Thank you, Lord, In Jesus' name, amen.

Posted on Facebook October 16, 2011

Father God, thank you for this wonderful day of family, ministry, fellowship, marriage, food, fun, communication and relaxation. Bless and protect my family and FB friends and restore and refresh my Pastors and all who was a part of Strategies 2011. Be glorified in my life. Thank you, Lord! God, you're faithful. I love, honor and adore You! In Jesus' name, amen. Have a favor-filled day of worship and word all!

Posted on Facebook October 19, 2011

Father God, thank you for Your faithfulness towards me and my family. Great is Your mercy and grace. Guide my steps, attitude, and actions. Be glorified in my life. I lift up my family and FB friends and pray that You minister to their need for salvation, strength, peace, joy, faith, comfort, healing, finances, favor and restoration. Thank you, Lord. In Jesus' name. Amen. Have a blessed day family and FB friends!

Posted on Facebook October 19, 2011

Father God, I lift up Pastor Youcef Nadarkhani and his family to and pray Your perfect will be done in and through their lives. I plead the blood of Jesus over them. Demonstrate your power and save souls and lives through his faith in You. Thank you, Lord. In Jesus' name. Amen.

Posted on Facebook October 21, 2011

Grateful! Father God, I thank you for my life. I thank you that no matter what I may think could be better there is always someone with a challenge worse than me. I lift up my family and FB friends and pray that You move in their lives. Comfort those experiencing the loss of a loved one. Heal the physically, emotionally and mentally challenged. Provide finances and resources for those experiencing lack. Strengthen those experiencing frustration and discouragement. Thank you, Lord, for You are faithful. In Jesus' mighty name I pray with thanksgiving, amen. Be blessed today family and FB Friends! God can be trusted. Lean on Him!

Posted on Facebook October 21, 2011

Father God, I lift up President David Wilson, my Morgan State family and the family of Julian Benson and pray for your presence to surround them during this tragic loss. Saturate the campus with peace that passes all understanding. Heal hearts and minds like only You can. Minister to their hurt right now. Thank you, Lord. In Jesus' name, amen. Much love family!

Posted on Facebook November 3, 2011

Father God, I thank you for this new day. I declare peace and productivity over my day and that everyone and everything including me cooperate with the plans and purposes You have ordained for my life. I take authority over my environment and atmosphere and come against frustration and distractions In Jesus' name. Order my steps. Use me for Your glory. Thank you, Lord! In Jesus' name. Amen. Have a blessed day family and FB friends!

Posted on Facebook November 4, 2011

Father God, thank you for this fantastic day. I will be focused and productive in it. Thank you for Your faithfulness to me and my family and friends. I love You Lord and am grateful for Your love, mercy, and grace. In Jesus' name, amen. Have a blessed, favor-filled day family and FB friends! Be safe!

Posted on Facebook November 6, 2011

Thankful for the extra hour. Father God, I pray for a life-changing, heart-searching, encouraging, convicting worship service across the nation where members and guests alike in attendance who are called by Your name would humble ourselves, pray, seek Your face and turn from our wicked ways so that You would hear from heaven, forgive our sin and heal our land. Revive us again. Thank you, Lord. In Jesus' name. Amen.

Posted on Facebook November 7, 2011

Father God, I thank you for this new day. I pray for order and direction for my day. I decree that limitations are broken and everyone and everything cooperates with Your plans and purpose for my life. I speak peace and productivity over my day and come against frustrations. Touch, heal, encourage, comfort, save, strengthen and deliver my family and FB friends. Thank you, Lord. In Jesus' mighty name. Amen.

Posted on Facebook November 9, 2011

Father God, thank you for satisfying me and my family with a long, abundant life and showing us Your salvation. I declare and decree breakthrough and prosperity over our lives. We prosper in our relationships, our health, our finances. We are Kingdom financiers. We shall live and declare the glory of God. Thank you for victory and favor! In Jesus' name, amen.

Posted on Facebook November 9, 2011

Father God, I thank you for this day that You made. I speak peace, order and productivity into and over my day. Everyone cooperates with Your plans and purpose for me and my family. I walk in increase and abundance for I am a Kingdom financier and builder. Limitations are broken and frustrations cease. I shall live and declare the glory of God. Hallelujah! Thank you, Lord. In Jesus' name. Amen. Have a blessed day family and FB friends!

Posted on Facebook November 10, 2011

Father God, thank you for the water-walking experiences that have forever changed my life. Thank you for blessing me and enlarging my territory. Thank you for being with me and keeping me from evil that I may not cause pain. Thank you for forgiveness and favor. Thank you for salvation and security. Thank you, Lord! In Jesus' name. Amen. Be blessed family and FB friends!

Posted on Facebook November 11, 2011

Father God, I lift up the USA and the world and plead the blood of Jesus over it and us. I pray for protection only You can provide. I pray that we would humble ourselves, pray, seek your face and turn from our wicked ways so that You would hear from heaven, forgive our sins and heal our land. I lift up our veterans and families. Bless and heal them. Thank you for our armed forces. Strengthen and fortify it. In Jesus' name. Amen.

Posted on Facebook November 12, 2011

Father God I thank you for this week. It was along week, and I am grateful for today. Thank you for peace, provision, and protection. Thank you for grace and mercy. Thank you for love and forgiveness. Thank you for freedom to worship. I am grateful for Pastors that love You and live the Word and a church family in which to serve and grow. Bless my family, church family, and friends and move in our lives. I pray for the lost, hurting, depressed and discouraged. Heal, save, comfort, strengthen and set free. Thank you, Lord. In Jesus' mighty name I pray and with thanksgiving, amen.

Posted on Facebook November 14, 2011

Father God, I thank you for this new day of grace and mercy. Thank you for provision of peace and protection. Order my steps, guide my actions and may my attitude be pleasing to You. Bless my family and FB friends and break limitations today. Demonstrate Your power and open doors in the lives of my LPCC family member as we partner in WOW week. Stretch us and use us for Your glory. Thank you, Lord! In Jesus' mighty name. Amen.

Posted on Facebook November 16, 2011

Heavenly Father, thank you for this new day of mercy and grace You have made! Thank you for the sacrifice of your Son and His shed blood for my sins. I am completely forgiven, greatly blessed and highly favored. Order my steps and use me for Your glory. Bless, heal, comfort, strengthen and deliver my family and FB friends this day! Thank you, Lord! In Jesus' name, amen. Have a wonderful Wednesday!

Posted on Facebook November 17, 2011

Father God, You are faithful, and I thank you for loving me even with my imperfections. I lift up my family, FB friends and colleagues and pray that You would bless them in their every need – a sound mind, healing in their body, favor with the courts and financial institutions, strength to stand and boldness to move, peace and comfort over the loss of a loved one, encouragement to know they can trust You, restoration of hurt relationships. You see them and know them. Thank you, Lord! In Jesus' name, amen. Have a blessed day all!

Posted on Facebook November 18, 2011

Corporate prayer is a great way to start the day. Father God, thank you for another day. Order my steps and use me for Your glory. Bless my family and FB friends with health, strength, peace, protection, favor and finances. Heal, comfort and encourage those in need. God, You are faithful and can be trusted. Thank you, Lord. In Jesus' name, amen. Have a fantastic Friday all!

Posted on Facebook November 18, 2011

Father God, I thank you for Your continued faithfulness to my family, FB friends, and Pastors and church family. I stand still expecting to see Your salvation on our behalf. I believe we receive everything You ordained for our lives. Thank you for increase and overflow. Thank you for provision and protection. I love, honor and adore You, Lord. In Jesus' name. Amen.

Posted on Facebook November 30, 2011

Father God I lift up Billy Graham and pray for healing in his body. I pray for accurate diagnosis and treatment and come against mistakes or mishaps. Continue to use him to draw souls to You. Thank you for satisfying him with long life. Minister through him to those around him. Bless him and his family. In Jesus' name, amen.

Posted on Facebook Friday, December 2, 2011, 8:06 am

Father God, I thank you for this new day You have made. I am glad and rejoice in it. I pray it's a productive day free of frustration. I pray for peace that passes all understanding. I lift up my family and FB friends and pray that You bless their day – heal, comfort, strengthen, deliver, encourage, save. I thank You, God for Your continued faithfulness. There is no one like You Lord. In Jesus' name, I pray, amen. Happy Friday!!!

Posted on Facebook Friday, December 5, 2011

Father God, help me to be patient, pleasant, peaceful and productive this day, this week, this month. Thank you, Lord! In Jesus' name. Amen.

Posted on Facebook December 13, 2011, 5:56 am

Father God, thank you for this new day. Order my steps and be glorified in my life. I lift up my family and FB friends and pray that You save, heal, comfort, strengthen, encourage, deliver and restore those in need. You know them and see them right where they are. I pray they seek You first. Thank you, Lord, for Your faithfulness! In Jesus' name. Amen. Have a great day!

Posted on Facebook December 15, 2011

Father God, comfort all who've experienced a sudden loss of a family member. Surround the loved ones with Your peace and encourage all hearts. Thank you, Lord. In Jesus' name, amen.

Posted on Facebook December 31, 2011

Father God, take authority over every area of my life. In Jesus' name. Amen

2012

Thank you, Lord, for a productive day. Please, give me sweet sleep that I may wake rested and refreshed and ready for another day of marriage, mothering, making a living, ministry, mentoring and me.

Posted on Facebook January 6, 2012

Father God, this is the day You have made, and I rejoice and am glad in it. Prayers have gone forth and continue to be lifted. I thank You that You watch over Your word to perform it. I thank you for satisfying me with long life and showing me Your salvation. I thank you for the supernatural and miraculous at work in my life even now. I lift up my family and FB friends and pray that You move in their lives. You are faithful God and I trust You! I come against fear and frustration and declare favor surrounds me this day. Arise and demonstrate Your power on my behalf and in my life. Thank you for my Pastors and church family. Move like only You can in our lives this month that we would be forever changed. In Jesus' mighty name, amen! Have a fantastic, favor-filled Friday, and a wonderful weekend family and FB friends!

Posted on Facebook January 7, 2012

Grateful for the prayers and visits of my church family. Yesterday Elder George Wright's presence waiting with Robert was timely. My two prayer warrior sisters just ended a wonderful visit with powerful prayer. Love you Ministers Phyllis Saucier and Marjorie Kisuule. God is faithful!

Posted on Facebook January 7, 2012

More wonderful visits with laughter and powerful prayers. Thank you, Lord, for Drea, Sheri, Pastors Ayers, Pastor Laura, Elder John and Janelle! Father God, give me sweet sleep and rest tonight. May I have a great report to be released tomorrow. Body, do what you need to do. Thank you, Lord! In Jesus' name! Amen

Posted on Facebook January 8, 2012

Father God, you are faithful, and I continue to trust You. I thank you for bringing me through a successful surgery and for Supernatural healing taking place even now. Lord, grow me in You during this time of recovery. Use me to bless others as You continue to bless me. Demonstrate Your power in my life. Bless my family and FB friends. I love You and Thank You, Lord. In Jesus' name, amen. Your daughter!

Posted on Facebook January 9, 2012

Father God, help me to see life's interruptions as divine appointments from You and always to embrace the opportunities each one brings. Thank you, Lord!

Posted on Facebook January 12, 2012

Dear Heavenly Father, I lift up my family and pray for traveling mercies and a good weekend attending the memorial service for Papa. Show them favor going and coming. I come against delays, malfunctions and accidents in the air and on the ground. Minister to and encourage the entire Besteda family. Manifest Your presence to heal, save and restore. Bless Robert and the girls. Thank you, Lord, in advance! In Jesus' name. Amen.

Posted on Facebook January 12, 2012

Father God, You promise never to leave us or forsake us. I thank you that You're a very present help in time of need.

Posted on Facebook January 13, 2012

Father God, I lift up the corporate prayer on tonight and pray that You bless everyone who will lead in prayer, exhort and attend. I thank you in advance for the fruit that will come forth. Bless my Pastors and church family. I pray that today is a frustration-free, favor-filled Friday for them and all my family and FB friends. You are our peace, joy, strength and salvation. I love you and thank you, Lord! In Jesus' name, I pray. Amen.

Posted on Facebook January 16, 2012

Father God, as I close my eyes to go to sleep, give me sweet, uninterrupted rest and may I wake refreshed. Thank you for wonderful worship and word via Cyber Church today. As we've already prayed, thank you for traveling mercies for my family's return home. In Jesus' name, amen. Goodnight, family and FB friends

Posted on Facebook January 17, 2012

Father God, I thank you that as I close my eyes this night, Robert and the girls are back home safe and sound. Rest them tonight after a long travel day. Lord, I lift up our WOVEN Revival on Thursday and Friday. Arise and demonstrate Your power each night. Bless the planners, speakers, PMT workers and attendees. Bless our Pastors and church family. Thank you, Lord. In Jesus' name, amen.

Posted on Facebook January 18, 2012

Dear Heavenly Father, I thank you for this new day! I thank you that this headache leaves my body now. I thank you that today will be an even better day than yesterday. I thank you for shelter and provision. I thank you that all my needs are met. I thank you for a sound mind and your saving grace. Thank you for my family and FB friends. In Jesus' name, I pray with thanksgiving. Amen. Have a wonderful Wednesday all!

Posted on Facebook January 19, 2012

God is my protector, my restorer, my healer, my provider, my comforter, my Savior, my peace, my joy, my strength, my strong tower, my refuge, my all.

Posted on Facebook January 20, 2012

Father God, I thank you for this day just starting for my east coast and island peeps. Bless them and give them a favor-filled Friday. Do the same for my west coast folks and everyone in between when we begin our day. Show up and show out in the lives of your people in a mighty way today. Thank you, Lord! In Jesus' name, amen. God is faithful, and can be trusted!

Posted on Facebook January 21, 2012

Father God, thank you for this new day! Thank you for breath, health and strength. Thank you for mercy and grace. Bless this day. I pray for safe travels for those who must be out in the rain or snow. God, You are faithful! I love and trust You! In Jesus' name, amen. Have a wonderful weekend family and FB friends!

Posted on Facebook January 23, 2012

Father God, thank you for my loving, caring, supportive husband. I pray that You move in and through His life. May he walk in wisdom and discernment. Holy Spirit, fill him up to overflowing. I love him, and I love You, Lord! In Jesus' name, amen.

Posted on Facebook January 27, 2012

Father God, I thank you for this new day. I praise You for You are faithful. I love, honor and adore You. I appreciate my life and the breath, health and strength You give me daily. Thank you for the love and support of my family and friends! Bless my family and FB friends this day! Use me for Your glory! Thank you, Lord! In Jesus' name, amen. Have a fantastic, favor-filled Friday family and FB friends!

Posted on Facebook January 30, 2012

Father God, You are my Rock, Strong Tower and Shield. I lift up my family, FB friends and church family who may have winds raging in their lives and pray You strengthen and anchor them. Whether they're experiencing the sickness of a loved one, loss of employment, a death of a friend or family member, or another catastrophic occurrence, minister to them right where they are in need. Thank you, Lord! In Jesus' name, amen.

Posted on Facebook February 1, 2012

Father God, I thank you for Your mercy and grace and forgiveness and faithfulness. I thank you for bringing us into another month. I pray that You go before us to make crooked places straight. I pray Your favor surrounds us and Your blessings overtake us. Bless us to be a blessing. Demonstrate Your power on our behalf. We can do all things through Christ who strengthens us. Heal the sick. Save the lost. Comfort the grieving. Encourage the depressed. Minister to the needs of Your people. Thank you, Lord! In Jesus' mighty name, amen!

Posted on Facebook February 9, 2012

Father God, I lift up the Thorough good family and New Jerusalem church and pray for Your peace, comfort, and strength to surround them. Encourage their hearts and heal their hurts. In Jesus' name, amen.

Posted on Facebook February 11, 2012

Dear Heavenly Father, thank you for salvation, security, soundness of mind and a support system. Lord, I lift up Whitney's mom, daughter and family to You right now and pray for Your presence to surround them and comfort them. Speak peace and calm to their minds and hearts. Lord God, begin the healing process in their lives and help them through the next hours and days. Thank you, Lord. You are faithful! In Jesus' name, amen.

Posted on Facebook February 18, 2012

Father God, I lift up my family and FB friends and pray that You move in their lives right now. Heal, save, encourage, comfort, strengthen now. You Lord God are a present help. Help those in need right now. Touch hearts, minds, bodies, emotions right now. You see everything and everyone. Manifest Your presence right now. Thank you, Lord, for Your faithfulness. In Jesus' mighty and matchless name. Amen!

Posted on Facebook February 21, 2012

Father God, I take authority over this day and decree and declare it will be peaceful, productive, favor-filled and frustration-free. I come against distractions In Jesus' name. Order my steps and make crooked places straight. I am grateful for Your grace and mercy. Be glorified in my life. Thank you for complete healing. Bless my family and FB friends. In Jesus' matchless name I pray with thanksgiving, amen. Have a great day!

Posted on Facebook February 28, 2012

Dear Heavenly Father, thank you for another day of life, breath, health and strength. Lord, I pray for protection over our homes, schools and workplaces and come against death, destruction and confusion. Heal, comfort, encourage and bless my family, Pastors and church family and FB friends. I decree and declare peace and productivity over my day and that it will be frustration free and favor-filled. Thank you, Lord God for hearing and answering. In Jesus' mighty name, amen. Have a great day all!

Posted on Facebook February 29, 2012

Thank you, Father God for this new day. I decree and declare peace, order and productivity over my day. I come against frustration and distractions in the name of Jesus. Lord God, order my steps and orchestrate my activities. Thank you for hearing and answering. In Jesus' name. Amen. Have a fruitful, favor-filled day family and FB friends. I certainly will!

Posted on Facebook March 1, 2012

Father God, thank you for this wonderful reminder to always consult You and the example of what happens when we don't. You can always be trusted. Thank You, Lord, for this new day of new grace and mercy. I trust You with all my heart. Help me not to lean on my understanding. Direct my paths as I acknowledge You in all my ways. I decree and declare peace and productivity over my day. Bless, protect, comfort, heal, encourage, strengthen and provide for the needs of my family and FB friends! God, You, are beyond awesome and I Thank You for who You are. Thank You for your love, compassion and forgiveness. In Jesus' mighty name, amen.

Posted on Facebook March 5, 2012

Dear Heavenly Father, thank you for this new day of grace and mercy. I lift up my household, family, FB friends and Pastors and church family and pray for blessings to overflow in their lives. I pray for peace, healing, favor, strength, joy, soundness of mind, comfort, encouragement and financial breakthrough. May we feel Your tangible presence today. Thank you, Lord, for hearing and answering. In Jesus' matchless name. Amen.

Posted on Facebook March 5, 2012

I decree and declare peace, productivity, favor and fruitfulness over my day. Everyone and everything, myself included, cooperates with the plans and purposes that God has ordained for my life. I come against frustration and distractions in the name of Jesus. I walk in destiny this day, this week, this month, this year. Greater is He Who is working in me than he who is working in the world. Thank You, Lord God!

Posted on Facebook March 6, 2012

Dear Heavenly Father, thank you for this new day. I lift up my family and FB friends and pray You bless them with peace, health, favor, strength, joy, soundness of mind, comfort, encouragement and finances. I decree and declare peace, productivity, favor and fruitfulness over my day. I come against frustration and distractions in the name of Jesus. Thank you, Lord, for hearing and answering. In Jesus' matchless name. Amen.

Posted on Facebook March 12, 2012

Father God, I thank You for this new day. Lord, I am fearfully and wonderfully made, created in Your image and I choose to walk in the authority and anointing You've empowered and equipped me with. Be glorified in and through my life. I decree and declare order, peace and productivity over my day, week and month. They will be frustration-free and favor-filled. Bless my family and FB friends. Thank you, Lord, for hearing and answering. In Jesus' name, amen. Let's finish this quarter strong!

Posted on Facebook March 13, 2012

Father God, I lift up to You my Pastors, Dr. Fred and Pastor Linda Hodge, and thank You for calling them to and equipping them for Kingdom building. I celebrate their faithfulness and fruit. Give them the desires of their heart as they continue to delight in You. Bless, protect and direct them. I pray for the entire body of Christ to that the uncompromised Word of God would be taught and lived so that real and lasting change would result. Hear from heaven, forgive our sin and heal our land. Thank you, Lord! In Jesus' mighty name, amen.

Posted on Facebook March 17, 2012

Amazing, the shooter has not been arrested because...? Father God, please comfort the family and friends of Trayvon Martin with your presence that brings the peace that passes all understanding. God, encourage them and help them through this process. Meet their needs as their lives have now been turned upside down. Show them favor with everyone they come in contact. Heal hearts and hurts. Thank you, Lord! In Jesus' name, amen.

Posted on Facebook March 18, 2012

Father God, I thank you for this new day, new year, new season. I embrace all that You have planned for me. Work in me and through me for Your glory. Thank you, Lord God for Your continued faithfulness in my life. Thank you for my family, my Pastors and church family and friends! I trust You, Lord! In Jesus' mighty, matchless and powerful name I pray. Amen.

Posted on Facebook March 19, 2012

Dear Heavenly Father, Thank You for the blessing of another birthday. I am grateful for another year of life and look forward with great anticipation and excitement to live it out and declare Your works. You are faithful. I decree and declare peace and productivity over my day. It is absolutely favor-filled and frustration-free. Be glorified in and through my life. I love you, Lord! In Jesus' name! Amen!

Posted on Facebook March 21, 2012

Father God, I thank you for this new day. Order my steps and orchestrate my day. I decree and declare peace, productivity and protection over my day that only Your presence can provide. Thank you for Your continued faithfulness and unfailing love and forgiveness. May this day be fruitful and favor-filled. Bless my family and FB friends. Be glorified in my life. Thank you, Lord, for hearing and answering. In Jesus' name. Amen! Have a dynamic day family and FB friends!

Posted on Facebook March 27, 2012

Father God, I thank you for this new day that You have made and the start of NCT 2012. I pray for favor throughout this entire event and traveling mercies. Bless our families. I decree and declare peace, order and productivity over this day and event. I come against frustration and distractions. I thank you, Lord, for your continued faithfulness! In Jesus' mighty name I pray, Amen.

Posted on Facebook March 27, 2012

Father God, thank you for a peaceful and productive workday with the safe arrival of everyone scheduled. Now give me sound sleep that I may wake on time, rested and refreshed to have another dynamic day. Bless my family and FB friends and protect us through the night for You neither slumber nor sleep. Thank you, Lord! In Jesus' name. Amen. Good night!

Posted on Facebook March 28, 2012

Great is God's faithfulness. Father God, thank you for this day. Order my steps Lord and line everything and everyone up with Your plans. I decree and declare peace, productivity, favor and fruitfulness. I come against critical thinking and communication and frustration and demonic interference. I plead the blood of Jesus over my family and friends and pray for healing and protection this day. Thank you, Lord. In Jesus' name. Amen.

Posted on Facebook March 28, 2012

Father God, thank you for the end of a productive workday and safe arrival of everyone scheduled today. Watch over us as we sleep. Give me a sound, restful night that I may wake rested in the morning. I pray for traveling grace for everyone arriving tomorrow. Bless my family and FB friends. In Jesus' name. Amen.

Posted on Facebook March 29, 2012

Dear God, I'm grateful that all NCT volunteers arrived in LA safely and with all the great dedication was working well into the night. Rest them well tonight Lord. Father God, I pray for traveling mercies with no delays, flight cancellations or emergencies for all the teams headed to LA. In Jesus' name. Amen.

Posted on Facebook March 30, 2012

This is the day the Lord has made. Hallelujah! Father God, pray for strength, stamina, energy and endurance for this day and weekend. Thank you, Lord for order and peace. Lord, answer the prayers of my family and friends for supernatural intervention, healing, deliverance, turnaround and breakthrough this day. Show up and show out. You are faithful and we trust you. Thank you, Lord! In Jesus' name. Amen.

Posted on Facebook April 1, 2012

Dear Lord, please give me such sweet sleep that the few hours I get would feel like I've had 8 hours when I wake. Strengthen and energize me for the day. Build up my immune system. Bless my Pastors and church family. I celebrate in advance what You will do through us as we sow our First Fruits. I wait with expectancy on the praise report. Bless Robert and the girls. Thank you, God. In Jesus' name. Amen

Posted on Facebook April 1, 2012

Dear God, thank you for Supernatural strength that truly kept me going all day on little sleep. You are faithful. Continue to keep me. In Jesus' name. Amen

Posted on Facebook April 3, 2012

Dear Heavenly Father, thank you for another day. I praise you God for a successful, NCT weekend. I pray for safe travel both in the air and on the ground for everyone leaving HCASC. Give them favor along the way. Order the activities of this day. Bless my family and FB friends. I decree and declare peace and productivity over this day. Thank you, Lord. In Jesus' name, amen.

Posted on Facebook April 9, 2012

Father God, thank you for this new day. Order my steps. Guide my thoughts. Direct my talk. I decree and declare peace and productivity over my day and come against frustration and distractions. Bless my family and FB friends. Heal their heart, mind and body. Heal their finances, emotions and relationships. You are faithful and more than able. Thank you, Lord! In Jesus' name. Amen

Posted on Facebook April 16, 2012

Father God, Thank You for this day. Thank You for the opportunity to celebrate my dad's birthday. Thank You for continuing to satisfy him with long, healthy, abundant life. Thank You for a wonderful and powerful weekend of worship, prayer and praise. I decree and declare peace and productivity over my day and I come against frustration and distractions. Bless my family, friends, Pastors and church family. In Jesus' name, amen.

Posted on Facebook April 17, 2012

Father God, Thank You for this new day. I decree and declare peace and productivity over my day and I come against frustration and distractions. I bind my mind to the mind of Christ. Holy Spirit, give me discernment for necessary decisions. Bless my family and friends. In Jesus' name, amen.

Posted on Facebook April 18, 2012

Father God, I thank You for another day. I decree and declare peace, order and productivity over my day and come against frustration, distraction and confusion. Satan, I serve you notice that you do not have the victory. Thank you, Lord, for a fruitful, favor-filled day! Bless me to be a blessing.

Today is the day that You made. In the mighty, matchless name of Jesus, I pray. Amen. Have a wonderful Wednesday family and FB friends!

Posted on Facebook April 20, 2012

Father God, I thank you for this new day that You have made! I am grateful for the blessing of life, health, strength, and soundness of mind. I decree and declare, peace, order, productivity, favor, and breakthrough over my day and my family. I/We walk in victory in every area. I come against confusion and distractions. Bless, heal, comfort, deliver, save and strengthen my family and FB friends. Thank you, Lord, for hearing and answering. In Jesus' name, I pray, amen. It's FRIDAY!!!!!!!!!! Have a fantastic day all!

Posted on Facebook April 22, 2012

Father God, thank you for this new day. Minister in every service today, touch hearts and minds and heal bodies. Bless those who must work today and miss worship. Thank you for Your forgiveness and Your faithfulness. In Jesus' mighty name, amen.

Posted on Facebook April 24, 2012

Father God, thank you for this day. I pray for safety for everyone traveling by plane, train or automobile to WWW in Houston this week. Bless all the participants and attendees. I lift up Pastor Linda and my LPCC family. I decree and declare peace and order, favor and fruitfulness over my day. I come against distraction and confusion. Heal, comfort and strengthen my family and FB friends in need. Thank you, Lord. In Jesus' name. Amen.

Posted on Facebook April 25, 2012

Father God, I thank you for this day that You have made. I am glad, and I rejoice in it. This day is already blessed !I decree and declare PEACE,ORDER and FAVOR over my day ,my life and my family and come against confusion, deception, and distractions. Be glorified in my life. Orchestrate the activities of my day. Continue to bless the Women Who Win Conference! You are faithful, and I am grateful!

In Jesus' name, I pray with thanksgiving, amen. Have a wonderful Wednesday family and FB friends!

Posted on Facebook April 27, 2012

Father God, thank you for this day! Your compassions fail not. They are new every morning. Great is Your faithfulness! This day and everyone and everything in it will cooperate with Your plan for my life. Order my steps. Use me for your glory. Bless, heal and comfort my family and FB friends. In Jesus' name. Amen. Happy Friday!

Posted on Facebook April 29, 2012

Father God, I lift up my family and FB friends and pray for those who are overwhelmed by the challenges along their path. Grace them to walk through it and come out stronger. Have mercy on those who need mercy. Surround those in need with your love, peace and comfort. Heal physically, mentally, emotionally, relationally and financially. Thank you, Lord, for hearing and answering. In Jesus' name. Amen.

Posted on Facebook April 29, 2012

Father God, I thank you for this day You have made. I pray for a wonderful day of prayer, praise, worship and word in all services. I decree and declare peace, order and success over this day and come against confusion, frustration and distraction. Lord, be glorified in this day. Order my steps and surround me with favor. Thank you, Lord. In Jesus' name. Amen.

Posted on Facebook April 29, 2012

God, You are so faithful! Father, I lift up my Pastors, Dr. Fred Hodge and Pastor Linda Hodge to you. I bless You for their ministry to LPCC and the body of Christ. Demonstrate your power on their behalf. Be glorified in their lives. Thank you, Lord for hearing and answering! In Jesus' name.

Posted on Facebook April 30, 2012

Father God, I thank you for this day that You have made. I expect blessings of health, strength, soundness of mind, power, provision, peace, favor and fruitfulness to follow and surround me. Lord, use me to bless others. You are my Savior, Protector, Healer and Provider. Thank you for grace and mercy, love and forgiveness. Demonstrate your power this day. Thank you, Lord. In Jesus' name. Amen.

Posted on Facebook May 1, 2012

Father God, thank you for this new day, new month and new opportunity to make a change and a difference. Thank you for never leaving us or forsaking us. Thank you for peace, protection and provision. Thank you for forgiveness and favor. Thank you for health, strength and soundness of mind. Thank you for salvation and the promise of eternal life with you. Thank you. Thank you. Thank you. Move in the lives of my family and friends his day. In Jesus' name, amen.

Posted on Facebook May 3, 2012

Father God, I thank you that You're an ever present help. You promise never to leave us or forsake us. You encourage us to cast all our cares on You and trust in You with all our heart. You're our hope, joy, strength, peace, comfort, and salvation. You love us and want us to seek You first in everything. Discouragement and depression are not from You. Demonic influence is from the enemy of our soul. I lift up my family and FB friends and their family and friends and pray for healing that is only found in You. Thank you, Lord. In Jesus' name. Amen.

Posted on Facebook May 4, 2012

Dear Heavenly Father, I thank You for this new day You have made. Be glorified in and through my life today. I decree and declare peace, order and favor over my day and come against frustration, confusion and aggravation. Thank You, Lord, for Your continued faithfulness. Bless my family and FB friends. In Jesus' name. Amen.

Posted on Facebook May 7, 2012

Dear Heavenly Father, I thank you for and trust Your perfect timing. You are faithful to perfect all that concerns me. Thank you for this new season. Help me to be bold and courageous in who You've called me to be and diligent to do what You've called me to. Order my steps this day, week, month, year. Dwell in me and use me for Your glory and to carry out Your will. Thank you, Lord! In Jesus' name, amen.

Father God, thank you for this day that you have made. I expect the supernatural to operate in my life today. I decree and declare peace and order over my day and come against confusion and frustration. Thank you for this new season of increase, elevation, promotion and overflow. I can and will do all things through Christ who gives me strength. Bless my family and FB friends. In Jesus' name. Amen.

Father God, I thank you in advance that today is a peace-filled, favor-filled, drama-free day. Thank you for my new season. Bless, comfort, strengthen, heal, deliver, save and provide for my family and FB friends. Thank you, Lord! In Jesus' name. Amen.

Thank you, God for life, for breath, health, strength, salvation, protection, peace, provision, wisdom, discernment, forgiveness, favor, family, fruit, increase, elevation, for insight, power, authority, utterance, Godly examples and leaders, and breakthrough. Thank you, Lord. In Jesus' name. Amen.

Father God, I thank you for this new day and a new season. Great is Your faithfulness and Your mercy. Your compassion fails not for it is new every morning. I lift up my family and FB friends and pray that You meet their needs today. Comfort the bereaved, heal the hurting and the sick, save the spiritually lost, encourage the depressed and discouraged, speak peace to the confused, restore fractured and broken relationships, favor those unjustly accused, provide for those needing a breakthrough, protect those in a challenging situation. Lord, I love You and thank You! In Jesus' name, amen.

Posted on Facebook May 25, 2012

Father God, thank you for this new day, the final Friday of May. This year is flying. Help me to be a faithful steward of my time, talent and treasure. Help me to manage my relationships and resources well. Bless me to be a blessing to others. Use me for Your glory. Minister to the needs of my family and FB friends. Thank you, Lord. In ' mighty name, amen!

Posted on Facebook May 28, 2012

Father God, thank you for this day to rest, relax and reflect. Thank you for Your faithfulness, for life, health and strength. Thank you for those who've given their lives in service to our country. Encourage and comfort their family members. I pray for those traumatized by their service and pray for physical, emotional and mental healing. Protect those who still serve. Meet the needs of our veterans. In Jesus' name, amen.

Posted on Facebook June 3, 2012

Father God, thank you for this new day. Thank you for being a present help. You are faithful, and I am grateful. Order my steps this day and week. I thank you for wisdom for every decision and favor in every situation and encounter. Bless my family and FB friends. Heal, comfort, encourage, strengthen, save, deliver, provide for, rescue those in need. Thank you, Lord. In Jesus' name, amen.

Posted on Facebook June 4, 2012

Father God, I pray for protection over the many teens who will be celebrating high school graduations this week and next. I pray for wisdom and good judgment. Keep them from death and destruction. In Jesus' name, amen.

Posted on Facebook June 5, 2012

Father God, I thank you, Lord, for this day. I pray for peace, order and favor in this day and come against frustration and confusion. I thank you, Lord, in advance. In Jesus' name. Amen.

Posted on Facebook June 6, 2012

Father God, I thank you for this new day. I pray for traveling mercies and protection as I make my way east. I plead the blood of Jesus over every mode of transportation I will take and come against accidents, malfunctions, emergencies, and any delay or demonic attack. I decree and declare peace, order and favor over my day and week. Thank you, Lord, for hearing and answering. In Jesus' mighty name. Amen!

Posted on Facebook June 9, 2012

Father God, thank you for a productive day. Please give me sound sleep and multiply these 3 hours that it feels like 6 when I wake. May I be refreshed and energized and rise without hitting snooze. Work everything out tomorrow for our good and Your glory. Thank you, Lord! In Jesus' name, amen.

Posted on Facebook June 11, 2012

Father God, thank you for this new day. It's been a great time celebrating with family and friends. I pray for protection, peace and favor to go before and with me as I make my way back from this short visit. I come against accidents, malfunction, distractions and confusion in Jesus' name. Bless my family and FB friends. Order my steps throughout this day. I thank you for safe travels. In Jesus' name. Amen. Happy and Blessed day!

Posted on Facebook June 12, 2012

Father God, thank you for this new day. Thank you for fellowship with family on both coasts. I pray for guidance and direction today. May my attitude and actions be pleasing to You. You are faithful, and I am grateful! Bless my family and FB friends! In Jesus' name, amen!

Posted on Facebook June 12, 2012

Father God, I lift up Robin Roberts and pray for accurate treatment and complete recovery and healing. I come against mistakes, mishaps, and complications for both her and her sister. Jehovah Rapha, demonstrate your power in her life. Thank you, Lord. In Jesus' name, amen.

Posted on Facebook June 18, 2012

Father God, I come against the spirit of death and destruction in Chicago and plead the blood of Jesus over that city. I also pray for healing in our land. Thank you, Lord In Jesus' name, amen.

Posted on Facebook June 20, 2012

Father God, thank you for this new day. Thank you for breath, health, strength, sight, hearing and soundness of mind. Thank you for loving and forgiving me. Order my steps and use me to be a blessing to my neighbor. Bless my family and FB friends. Thank you for peace, productivity and protection. Thank you that my day is full of favor and free of frustration, confusion, and stress. Thank you, Lord. In Jesus' name, amen.

Posted on Facebook June 23, 2012

Father God, thank you for this new day. Thank you for never leaving or forsaking me. You are faithful, and I trust You. I pray for peace, productivity and protection over my day. I come against frustration and confusion and thank you for favor. Bless my family and FB friends this day. Use me to be a blessing to others. Thank you, Lord. In Jesus' name. Amen

Posted on Facebook June 27, 2012

Father God, thank you for this new day. Thank you for Your constant care and compassion. I lift up my family and FB friends and pray that You meet their needs: salvation to the lost soul, peace to the troubled mind, comfort to the grieving heart, healing to the physically hurting, restoration to the broken, strength to the discouraged, finances to those lacking. Thank you, Lord. In Jesus' name, amen.

Posted on Facebook June 27, 2012

Father God, I pray for the 'Monster' Colorado fire to be quickly extinguished, for there to be no loss of life and further destruction. I pray for strength, energy, and endurance for the firefighters and the families affected. Demonstrate Your power in this situation. Thank you, Lord. In Jesus' name, amen.

Posted on Facebook June 28, 2012

Father God, thank you for traveling mercies. I pray for a fun, favor-filled family weekend of rest, relaxation and much enjoyment. I decree and declare peace and order over and around us and come against confusion, frustration, accidents or sickness. Thank you for protecting here and there. Bless our Family and FB friends! Thank you, Lord! In Jesus' mighty name. Amen.

Posted on Facebook July 1, 2012

Father God, thank you for a great 1st six months of 2012. I pray for an even better next six months. I pray to be spiritually, physically, financially, mentally and relationally healthier. I pray for success in marriage, mothering, ministry, work and business. I can do all things through Christ who strengthens me. Thank you, Lord, for strength, confidence, determination and discipline to finish strong. In Jesus' name, amen.

Posted on Facebook July 3, 2012

Father God, I pray for no loss of life from that Palmdale fire. I pray for the firefighters and all rescue personnel on duty. Strengthen them. I speak peace to the winds that they may cease to allow for the fire to be put out. Thank you, Lord. In Jesus' name. Amen.

Posted on Facebook July 8, 2012

Father God, I lift up our troops/veterans who have been diagnosed with PTSD and their family and friends who have been impacted. I pray for healing and that they all get the help they need for recovery. Restore all that's been lost. Thank you, Jehovah Rapha. In Jesus' name, amen.

Posted on Facebook July 15, 2012

Dear Heavenly Father, I thank You for your continued faithfulness. I praise You God for Your manifold blessings. I thank You for a fantastic family, powerful and passionate Pastors and a great church family in which to serve and grow. I stand still to see what You're going to do in and through my life. God, help me to manage marriage, mothering, ministry and myself well. Guide and grace me for every assignment.

Use me to be a blessing to others. Bless my family and FB friends. In Jesus' name, amen!

Posted on Facebook July 17, 2012

Father God, thank you for this new day. I decree and declare peace, order and favor over our day and come against confusion, frustration and demonic interference. I pray for protection over every mode of transportation we will take and for safe arrival at our destination. I pray the same for other family members traveling back. Bless my family and FB friends. Thank you, Lord. In Jesus' name. Amen.

Posted on Facebook July 24, 2012

Dear Heavenly Father, thank you for this new day. Thank you for fellowship with family and friends. Thank you for Your continued faithfulness over us. Guide us today and may we be a blessing to others as You are to us. Bless my family and FB friends. Thank you, Lord! In Jesus' name, amen!

Posted on Facebook July 26, 2012

Dear Heavenly Father, thank you for a fun time of fellowship with family and the ability to vacation at home. I pray for traveling mercies as were turn to our now home. I decree and declare peace, order and favor throughout the day and come against confusion, distraction, destruction and demonic interference. Thank you for safety in the van, plane, bus and car. Bless our family and FB friends. Prepare me as I return for this productive weekend. Thank you, Lord. In Jesus' name. Amen. Have a great day all!

Posted on Facebook July 28, 2012

Father God, I thank you for this new day. I thank you for this new season. Order my steps and direct my paths. Bless my family and FB friends. Strengthen me for the assignment and activities of this day and weekend. Thank you, Lord, for peace and favor. God, I trust You and love You. Thank you, for the wonderful fellowship with my WOVEN sisters. In Jesus' name, amen.

Posted on Facebook August 6, 2012

I decree and declare peace, protection, provision and promotion that comes from the presence of God over my day, week, month and year. I come against confusion, frustration, distractions, satanic attacks and demonic interference for I walk in dominion. This is my season and favor surrounds me. Thank you, Lord!

Posted on Facebook August 10, 2012

Father God, I need Your help. I need You to be my coach, trainer, and nutritionist. Jehovah Rapha, I thank You for healing my body before, during and through this process. Heavenly Father, give me the mental, physical and emotional strength to be successful. Lord, I thank You in advance for the realization of a healthy weight. I believe I can do all things through Christ who gives me strength. In Jesus' name. Amen. Determined. Inspired. Motivated. Encouraged.

Posted on Facebook August 14, 2012

Father God, thank you for the first day of school and another year of learning. I plead the blood of Jesus over Holmes Middle, Dearborn Elementary, and every public, private and parochial school in this nation. I pray for a safe, productive year and come against sexual perversion, satanic attacks, and all demonic interference. Cover every student and protect every school. May every student have success. Bless the administration, faculty and staff to have a great year and encourage and instruct with excellence. Thank you, Lord, for hearing and answering. In Jesus' name. Amen.

Posted on Facebook August 20, 2012

Father God, bless my niece Ciara on her first day of classes of the first year of her undergraduate experience at Morgan State today and my niece Brittany on her first day of classes next week of her last year of her undergraduate experience at Penn State. You have kept them and helped them to excel thus far. May they continue to have a successful life. Thank you, Lord. In Jesus' name, amen. Proud Auntie Tish

Posted on Facebook August 21, 2012

Dear Heavenly Father, thank you for this new day. Thank you for Your Holy Spirit who leads, guides and directs. I lift up my family and FB friends to You and pray that You minister to their need whether physical, financial, mental, emotional or relational. You are faithful God. Heal, comfort, encourage and surround them with Your peace right now. Thank you, Lord! In Jesus' name. Amen. Have a dynamic day!

Posted on Facebook August 24, 2012

Father God, I thank you for this day that You have made, and I rejoice and am glad in it. I decree and declare peace, protection, productivity and favor over this day and come against confusion, distraction, frustration and all satanic influence. I am expecting a supernatural, mighty move of God in my life and the lives of my family. You are faithful, and I trust You. In Jesus' matchless name. Amen!

Posted on Facebook August 26, 2012

Dear Heavenly Father, thank you for this new day. Thank you for freedom to worship You and gather corporately for prayer, praise and preaching. Bless my family and FB friends. Bless all services at Living Praise Christian Center today, and through Cyber Church that souls would be saved, lives would be forever changed, and hearts would be encouraged. Bless our Pastors Fred Hodge and Linda Hodge and the entire LPCC family. Thank you, Lord! In Jesus' name. Amen!

Posted on Facebook August 30, 2012

Dear Heavenly Father, thank you for this new day! Thank you for health, strength and soundness of mind. Thankful that You are greater than anything or anyone around me. Demonstrate Your power this day. Bless my family and FB friends. Save, heal, comfort, strengthen, deliver, restore, encourage, protect. You are faithful to Your promises and can be trusted. Thank you, Lord. In Jesus' name, Amen.

Posted on Facebook August 31, 2012

Dear Heavenly Father, thank you for this new day! Thank you for this tremendously blessed month of August. Thank you for manifestation of answered prayer and those that I have yet to see. Use me for Your glory. I expect a supernatural September and praise You in advance for the lives that will be changed, the hearts that will be encouraged, the souls that will be saved, the relationships that will be restored and the miracles, signs and wonders that will take place. Demonstrate your power, Lord. I thank you for peace, productivity, protection and favor. Bless my family and FB friends. I love, honor and praise You, God. In Jesus' name, I pray with thanksgiving. Amen.

Posted on Facebook September 1, 2012

Father God, thank you for this day You have made. Order our steps and bless our day. Give us success in our first yard sale and use us to be a blessing. Protect us and be glorified in and through us. I decree and declare peace, order and success over this day and come against confusion and all satanic interference. Bless my family and FB friends. Thank you, Lord. In Jesus' name. Amen.

Posted on Facebook September 2, 2012

Father God, I am overwhelmed with such a wonderful weekend. Yesterday was a great family day with everyone working our first yard sale together. Today was another great day of worship and word and nice family time. God, You are faithful, and I love You and thank you! Bless my family, FB friends, Pastors and church family and protect everyone traveling this Labor Day weekend. August was amazing. September will be sensational and October over-the-top. I am looking forward to my future in You. Be glorified in my life. Thank you, Lord! In Jesus' name, amen.

Posted on Facebook September 7, 2012

Father God, I thank you for this new day. Thank you for my church family Living Praise Christian Center and John Taylor and Stephanie Taylor for leading the prayer line. I am grateful for the blessing of being able to listen to this morning's recording. Thank you for the power of prayer.

Bless my Pastors, Dr. Fred and Linda Hodge this day. Bless my family and FB friends this day. Heal, strengthen, deliver, save, restore. Meet the needs of Your people. Thank you for peace, protection, provision, promotion and productivity. Thank you for salvation and security. You are my source, and I thank you for the resources You provide. Be glorified in and through my life. In Jesus' name, amen! Happy and Blessed Friday family!

Posted on Facebook September 7, 2012

Dear God, I thank you for life and helping me keep it in perspective. Comfort, strengthen and encourage everyone mourning the loss of a loved one whether last night, last week, last month or last year. Surround them with Your peace and love. Thank you, Jehovah Shalom. In Jesus' name. Amen.

Posted on Facebook September 11, 2012

Father God, thank you for this new day. I decree peace, order, and productivity over my day. I come against confusion, distractions, and frustration. Thank you for Your faithfulness and Your favor in my life and my family's lives. Bless, heal, save, deliver, comfort, strengthen, encourage and touch my family and FB friends in need right now. Thank you, Lord! In Jesus' mighty name. Amen.

Posted on Facebook September 13, 2012

Father God, I thank you for protection from dangers seen and unseen. I decree and declare peace, order, productivity and favor over this day and come against confusion, distractions, frustration and every satanic attack and demonic inference. No weapon formed shall prosper. My family, fitness, finances and future are blessed. Bless, encourage, comfort, heal, save, deliver, protect and promote my family, FB friends, and church family in need right now. Thank you, Lord! In Jesus' mighty and matchless name, Amen!

Posted on Facebook September 17, 2012

Dear Heavenly Father, thank you for Your sacrifice in the shed blood and broken body of Your Son Jesus Christ that through Him we may have forgiveness of sins and eternal life. Thank you for peace, protection, provision and promotion. Thank you for health, strength and soundness of mind. Thank you for salvation and security. I pray for physical, spiritual, financial, mental, relational and emotional healing and restoration in the lives of my family and FB friends. God, You are faithful. I trust You. Comfort and encourage those experiencing a loss. Demonstrate Your power in the lives of Your people this day. In Jesus' mighty and matchless name, I pray, amen.

Posted on Facebook September 22, 2012

Father God, I am so grateful for Your grace, love, mercy and forgiveness. I am blessed for my family by birth, marriage and my church family. I thank you for protection, provision, promotion and favor. I praise, honor and adore You. Thank you, Lord! In Jesus' name. Amen!

Posted on Facebook September 26, 2012

Father God, I thank you for my Pastors. Bless, strengthen, comfort and encourage Dr. Fred and Pastor Linda Hodge and the entire Hodge family. Move mightily in their lives. Thank you, Lord. In Jesus' name, amen.

Posted on Facebook September 28, 2012

Dear Heavenly Father, thank you for this day. I decree and declare peace, order, and favor over this day and come against confusion, satanic attack and demonic interference. Protect us from dangers seen and unseen and bless the activities and events of this day. Heal, comfort and encourage my family and FB friends. In Jesus' name. Amen. Happy Friday!

Posted on Facebook October 1, 2012

Dear Heavenly Father, thank you for this new day and new month. Thank you for peace, protection, provision, and promotion. Thank you for health, strength and a sound mind. Bless me to be a blessing. Help me to manage my relationships and resources well. Help me to be a good steward of my time, talent and treasure. Thank you for forgiveness and favor. Bless, heal, save, protect, comfort and encourage my family and FB friends. Thank you, Lord! In Jesus' name. Amen.

Posted on Facebook October 5, 2012

I am singing, Thank you, Lord, for giving me another chance, another chance to say thank you! Dear Heavenly Father thank you for this new day. Thank you for mercy, grace and forgiveness. I decree and declare peace, order, productivity and favor over this day and weekend. I come against confusion, frustration, accident, distraction, satanic attack and demonic interference. I pray for your protection over Morgan and all schools celebrating Homecoming this coming week. I pray that You bless, heal, save, comfort, encourage and deliver my family and FB friends. Bless my pastors and church family. Thank you, Lord. In Jesus' name, amen. Happy Friday!

Posted on Facebook October 11, 2012

Dear Heavenly Father, thank you for two nights of power-packed worship and word with so many wonderful ministry gifts. Thank you for planting me at LPCC in March 2004 under the leadership of two dedicated, dynamic Pastors. Thank you for opportunities to grow and mature. Bless my church family and use us to be a blessing. Restore and refresh everyone who served in any way for our 30/30 Conference and all those who were in attendance in person and via Cyber Church. Demonstrate Your power on our behalf. Thank you, Lord! In Jesus' mighty name I pray. Amen. I love my Pastors and church family!

Posted on Facebook October 13, 2012

Father God, I thank and praise You for You are beyond amazing, beyond awesome and so faithful. Thank you for never leaving or forsaking us. Thank you for this new day! I decree peace, order, and favor over this day and come against confusion, frustration, satanic attack and demonic interference especially over Morgan State University and that Northeast Baltimore community. Give them a fun day free of all negative occurrences. Bless, protect, save, encourage, comfort my family and FB friends. I love You and thank You, Lord. In Jesus' name. Amen. Have a wonderful weekend all and Happy Homecoming Morgan State! #MSU

Posted on Facebook October 18, 2012

Dear Lord, fill me with Your wisdom and Spirit. Let Your joy be my strength and Your peace prevail over all of my circumstances. Thank you! In Jesus' name, amen!

Posted on Facebook October 22, 2012

Dear Heavenly Father, I love You and thank You for another day to say thank You. I thank you for Your care and compassion. I thank you for Your favor, faithfulness, and forgiveness. I thank you for Your peace, protection, and provision. I thank you for Your salvation and security. Today I lift up a dear friend who I just found out is in intensive care receiving dialysis. Jehovah Rapha, demonstrate Your healing power in her body right now. By Jesus' stripes, she is healed. Bless my family and FB friends. Thank you, Lord! In Jesus' mighty and matchless name, I pray. Amen. Prayer warriors and my Morgan and Huber families, pray with me. Happy and Blessed Monday!

Posted on Facebook October 23, 2012

Father God, I thank you for healing every ache and pain in my body as a result of my falling off that machine at the start of my training tonight. I pressed through and finished strong because I have the victory. In Jesus' name, amen.

Posted on Facebook October 26, 2012

Father God, I thank you for this new day, the last Friday of October 2012. Thank you for breath, health and soundness of mind. Thank you for provision, protection and promotion. I declare peace, order and productivity over this day and weekend and come against confusion, frustration, satanic attack and demonic interference. Bless, save, heal, comfort, deliver, encourage my family and FB friends. Thank you, Lord. In Jesus' name. Amen. God is faithful. Trust Him!

Posted on Facebook October 28, 2012

Dear Heavenly Father, I thank you for a mighty yoke-destroying, burden-removing service today at LPCC. Thank you for healing hearts, minds, bodies and emotions. Thank you for the lives that were changed and relationships that were restored. Thank you for Your continued faithfulness. Now, God, I lift up the east coast and pray for Your protection and provision for everyone in the path of the storm. I speak peace to Hurricane Sandy. I pray everyone uses wisdom and are prepared. Demonstrate Your power, Lord. Thank you for hearing and answering. In Jesus' mighty and matchless name, I pray. Amen.

Posted on Facebook November 1, 2012

Dear Heavenly Father, thank you for this new day and new month. Thank you for breath in my body and soundness of mind. I lift up my family and FB friends and pray for their needs right now whether physical, spiritual, financial, emotional, mental or relational. Demonstrate Your power where it's a matter of life or death. Heal, comfort, encourage, strengthen, deliver, favor. Thank you, Lord. In Jesus' mighty name. Amen. Have a blessed day!

Posted on Facebook November 1, 2012

Father God, I lift up everyone impacted by Hurricane Sandy on both the east coast and in the Caribbean. I pray for quick recovery of services. I pray for resources needed for a return to normalcy. I pray for comfort and strength for everyone who lost a love done. Heal like only You can. Thank you, Lord. In Jesus' name. Amen.

Posted on Facebook November 5, 2012

Dear Heavenly Father, thank you for this new day. Thank you for new grace and mercy. Help me to be who You've called me to be and bless me to be a blessing. Thank you for peace, protection, provision and promotion. Order my steps and orchestrate my day. Thank you for my Pastors and church family and demonstrate Your saving, healing, restoring power through us. Bless, heal, comfort, deliver, encourage and save my family and FB friends this day. God, You are faithful and I trust You. Thank you, Lord. In ' mighty name, amen.

Posted on Facebook November 5, 2012

Dear Heavenly Father, I thank you for a great start to the work week. I lift up the elections on tomorrow and, pray for Your perfect will to be accomplished. I pray for everyone who holds positions of authority over us, both now and after the election. I pray for peace and order at the polls. I come against confusion and frustration. I pray that You demonstrate your power. Thank you for Your continued faithfulness. My confidence is in Christ, and I trust You, God! In Jesus' mighty and matchless name, I pray, amen. Be blessed!

Posted on Facebook November 6, 2012

A conversation I just had with a staff member at York College, CUNY made me tear up. They are a disaster site, and families are still 'living' in their facilities. She went in to the restroom, and a mother was cleaning up her two young daughters and getting them ready for bed. I am grateful for warm shelter in my home. Father God, heal the people impacted by Hurricane Sandy. Send help to ease the recovery. Encourage everyone displaced in any way by the storm. Touch hearts, minds, and spirits. Meet their needs. Thank you, Lord. In Jesus' name, amen.

Posted on Facebook November 7, 2012

Dear Heavenly Father which art in Heaven, hallowed be Thy name. I lift up the United States of America and pray for a much-needed healing in the land. I pray for healing of the anger, attitudes and even hate displayed during the campaign and still now. I lift up President Obama and the first family and pray for protection, strength and Godly wisdom to rule this country well. I pray for all elected officials to govern with integrity and with the people in mind. I come against greed and deceit. God, You are still on the throne, and Your mercy and grace still cover us. Thank you, Lord, for Your faithfulness and favor. In Jesus' name, I pray, amen.

Posted on Facebook November 9, 2012

Dear Heavenly Father, thank you for this new day and end of a work week for many. This has been an intense week in our country and a challenging one for many in the northeast. I lift up everyone going through a challenge whether physical, mental, financial, emotional, relational or spiritual. Heal, save, encourage, deliver, provide, strengthen and restore. Meet the needs of Your people. Renew hope. Rebuild trust. God, You are faithful. Thank you, Lord, for Your presence that brings peace, protection and provision. Thank you for salvation and security in You. I love, honor and adore you. In Jesus' name, amen. Happy and Blessed Friday family and FB friends.

Posted on Facebook November 19, 2012

Today is Jennifer's 13th birthday. We're taking her and a couple of friends ice skating. (Yep, I'll be watching:) Dear Heavenly Father, I pray for protection on the ice from accidents, falls, and all emergencies. Thank you, Lord. In Jesus' name. Amen.

Posted on Facebook November 21, 2012

Dear Heavenly Father, thank you for this new day. Thank you for Your mercy, grace, love and forgiveness. I lift up my family, FB friends and those not on FB and pray for protection and safe travels throughout this Thanksgiving holiday. I pray for good food and fellowship to be enjoyed. I pray for relationships to be restored. Save souls and lives. Heal hearts, minds and bodies. Bless physically, mentally, spiritually, relationally, emotionally and financially. Father God, you are faithful, and I trust You. Thank you for peace this day. In Jesus' name, amen. Happy Wednesday!

Posted on Facebook November 26, 2012

Father God, You are so awesome and amazing. You want the best for us. If we would only trust You and submit our will to Yours, we would see You move on our behalf. Bless, save, heal, comfort, protect, deliver and favor my family and FB friends. Thank you, Lord! I need and appreciate Your mercy, grace, love and forgiveness. In Jesus' name. Amen. Be blessed all!

Father God, thank you for this new day! Thank you for new mercy and grace. Thank you for health and strength. Thank you for family and friends. Heal Claudia Ruffin and Frank Pastore on this side of heaven and all those in need of a supernatural move of God in their bodies. I know you to be a healer so demonstrate Your power now Jehovah Rapha. I decree and declare peace, order and productivity over this day and come against confusion, frustration and all demonic attacks. Thank you, Lord, for favor, protection, provision and promotion. Bless my family and FB friends. In Jesus' mighty name. Amen

Father God, I give You the glory for the great things You've done and are yet doing. I expect souls to be saved, bodies to be healed, hearts to be encouraged, relationships to be restored and prayers to be answered. Thank you, Lord! You are faithful. You are awesome. You are amazing. In Jesus' name. Amen and Amen!

Father God, thank you for this new day. I am grateful for breath, health, strength and soundness of mind. Bless my family and FB friends. I decree and declare peace, order, productivity and favor over this day. I come against confusion, frustration, distraction and satanic influence. Thank you for wisdom and discernment. Use me to be a blessing. In Jesus' name. Amen.

Hallelujah! Glory to God! The God I serve is a Miracle Worker. He is a Healer, and He answers prayer! I just received a phone call from my friend we have been praying for Claudia Ruffin since October. She is out of ICU and out of the hospital. She is home. Hallelujah!

Father God, if I had 10,000 tongues, I couldn't praise You enough. I lift up Claudia to You for continued and complete healing. I pray for complete restoration of all function and ability daily. Continue to demonstrate Your power in her body and life. You are faithful God, and I love You and thank You! In Jesus' mighty, matchless and powerful name I pray. AMEN!!! Y'all don't know how I feel right now. Beyond Blessed!

Posted on Facebook December 6, 2012

Father God, I lift up everyone going through health challenges or anyone caring for someone going through health challenges. I pray for accuracy in diagnosis and treatment. I pray there be no infections or complications with any procedures or prescriptions. I pray for complete and quick physical, mental and emotional healing for the patient. I pray for physical and mental strength for all caregivers. Jehovah Rapha, demonstrate Your power. Lord, I also lift up everyone going through grief over a current death or anniversary of a death of a loved one. Comfort, strengthen and encourage them right now. Surround them with Your peace. Thank you, Lord. In Jesus' name, amen.

Posted on Facebook December 11, 2012

Father God, I lift up my great alma mater Morgan State and pray for stability and security. I pray that all parties act in the best interest of its students, faculty, staff and alumni. Demonstrate Your power and reveal the truth. Thank you, Lord! In Jesus' name, Amen. Fair Morgan Forever, Forever Morgan

Posted on Facebook December 12, 2012

Dear Heavenly Father, thank you for this dynamic day that You have made. Thank you for health, strength and wholeness. Thank you for peace, protection, provision and promotion. Thank you for family, friends, forgiveness and favor. Thank you for increase and elevation. Thank you for resources and relationships ordained by You. Thank you for wisdom and discernment. Thank you for vision and insight. Thank you for needs met and prayers answered. Thank you for the shed blood of your Son Jesus and the salvation and security it gives. Thank you for grace and mercy. Thank you for another chance to say thank you! I decree and declare this day that my fitness, family, and finances are blessed! I love you, Lord! In Jesus' name, amen!

Posted on Facebook December 14, 2012, 5:32 am

Dear Heavenly Father, which art in heaven, hallowed be thy name. Thank you for this new day. Thank you for watching over us and never leaving us or forsaking us. Thank you for peace, protection and provision. Thank you for salvation, safety and security. Order my steps and orchestrate my activities. Use me to be a blessing to others. Bless, heal, save, deliver, comfort, strengthen, encourage and restore my family and FB friends and their family members. Demonstrate Your power. Someone needs a supernatural move of God. Thank you, Lord! You are faithful and can be trusted. In Jesus' name. Amen. Happy Friday! Have a fantastic day!

Posted on Facebook December 17, 2012

Father God, as the funeral services for the CT shooting victims, begin, please comfort, strengthen and encourage every family member, friend, and the first responder. Heal every classmate, teacher, and parent. Heal that community and our country. I plead the blood of Jesus over our schools and communities in general. You are our only hope. Thank you, Lord, for hearing and answering. In Jesus' name, amen.

Posted on Facebook December 18, 2012

Dear Heavenly Father, as I hear about the death of Frank Pastore, I am grateful for life and do not take it for granted. I pray for strength and peace for his wife Gina, his entire family, and everyone who was ever impacted by his life I pray that souls would be saved and lives yet changed by his having lived. Comfort all those who mourn. Thank you, Lord. God, You are still faithful! I thank You and love You. In Jesus' name, amen.

Posted on Facebook December 31, 2012

Father God, thank you for a blessed 2012. Thank you for protection, provision and preservation. I pray that souls would be saved and lives forever changed in tonight's service. Bless every expression of ministry and may it give You glory. Demonstrate your power. I pray for traveling mercies as we make our way back home. Thank you, Lord. In Jesus' name. Amen.

2013

Posted on Facebook January 1, 2013

As we enter our home in this new year, I decree and declare peace, productivity, prosperity, promotion, increase, elevation, unity, favor, health, wealth, debt freedom and victory over our lives! I come against confusion, frustration, distraction, lack, sickness and every satanic attack or demonic interference. This is our year to possess all God has for us. The Rose family is blessed! Thank you, Lord!

Posted on Facebook January 2, 2013

Father God, as many of us return to work today or start a new job, I pray You go before us to protect and favor us. I pray for peace and productivity over our day. Heal those who are challenged and can't work right now and provide for those who are in need of work. Bless and protect all students returning to school today. Thank you, Lord. In Jesus' mighty name. Amen!

Posted on Facebook January 2, 2013

Father God, comfort all those grieving the death of a loved one whether today, last week, last month or last year. Encourage them and surround them with peace that passes all understanding. Walk with them through the healing process. Thank you, Lord. In Jesus' mighty name, amen.

Posted on Facebook January 3, 2013

Father God, thank you for this day that You have made. I decree and declare peace, order, productivity and favor over this day. I come against confusion, frustration, distractions and all demonic interference. Thank you for health, healing, wholeness and soundness of mind. Thank you for victory in every area. Thank you for protection throughout this day. Bless, save, heal, comfort, deliver, strengthen, encourage and provide for my family and FB friends. Thank you for Your continued faithfulness. In Jesus' mighty name. Amen!!!

Posted on Facebook January 7, 2013

Dear Heavenly Father, thank you for a new day and another work week. I lift up all students making their way back to school from elementary through college and plead the Blood of Jesus over them and pray for protection and productivity. I pray for a peaceful commute as more cars will be moving about. Order our steps this day. Be glorified in our lives this day. Use us to be a blessing this day. You are faithful, and I trust You. Thank you, Lord. In Jesus' name. Amen.

Posted on Facebook January 9, 2013

Dear Heavenly Father, thank you for this new day! I lift up those in need of Your healing touch. Be in the midst of any surgery taking place today. Accelerate the healing process of those out of surgery. Meet the needs during recovery. I lift up the bereaved. Comfort and encourage those experiencing a loss. Thank you, Lord. In Jesus' name. Amen.

Posted on Facebook January 9, 2013

Father God, I thank you for peace, protection, provision and preservation this day. Thank you for healing, saving and stopping the hand of the enemy. Thank you for the victory. You are faithful, and I trust You! In Jesus' mighty and matchless name, I pray. Amen. Be blessed family and FB friends.

Posted on Facebook January 13, 2013

Dear Heavenly Father, thank you for this blessed day. Thank you for rich worship and word at church this morning. Thank you for great fellowship this afternoon. Thank you for a peaceful and productive evening. Thank you for discipline and self-control. Thank you for blessing my family, fitness, finances and future. Thank you for favor and victory in every area of my life. Bless, save, heal, comfort, deliver, protect, strengthen, encourage and provide for my family and FB friends. Thank you, Lord! God, You are faithful and can be trusted. In Jesus' mighty name, amen.

Posted on Facebook January 14, 2013

Father God, I lift up Robin Roberts to You and pray for complete healing in her body, blood and bone marrow. I come against sickness, disease, infection and complication. Satisfy her with long, healthy life and show her Your salvation. Thank you, Lord, for Your healing power! In Jesus' mighty name, amen.

Posted on Facebook January 16, 2013

Father God, thank you for this new day. Thank you for blessing Your people with peace, provision and protection. This is the day that You have made, and we rejoice in it. We choose to be glad because You are faithful. Order our steps and orchestrate our activities and assignments. Be glorified in our lives and use us to bless others. Thank you, Lord! In Jesus' name. Amen. Happy Wednesday!!!

Posted on Facebook January 18, 2013

Dear Heavenly Father, thank you for a new day. Thank you for breath, health, strength and soundness of mind. I lift up my family and FB friends, my Pastors and church family and pray that You meet them at their place of need. You see, hear and care. Bless, heal, save, comfort, deliver, strengthen, encourage and provide for them. God, You are faithful. I pray for protection on land, in the air, and on the water. I pray for peace over this entire weekend, especially in our Nation's Capitol. God, show up and show out. Thank you, Lord. In Jesus' name. Amen.

Posted on Facebook January 18, 2013

Father God, I thank you that the victim thrown on the subway tracks wasn't seriously injured. I thank you, the suspect is in custody. Whatever mental challenges there are, heal him. Protect commuters everywhere. I come against copycat craziness. In Jesus' name, amen.

Posted on Facebook January 19, 2013

Dear Heavenly Father, I lift up everyone "going through something" right now. I pray for healing for those recovering from surgery. I pray for comfort for those experiencing the recent loss of a loved one. I pray for hope for those who feel like they can't go on. I pray for peace in the midst of confusion. I pray for provision for those that are on their last. I pray for employment for those who are seeking. I pray for restoration of broken relationships. God, You are so faithful. Thank you, Lord. In Jesus' mighty name. Amen.

Posted on Facebook January 22, 2013

Father God, bless, protect and favor my second niece who is starting her second semester at Morgan State. Thank you for a great Fall semester and help her to finish strong in May. God, You're faithful. In Jesus' name. Amen.

Posted on Facebook January 23, 2013

Dear Heavenly Father, thank you for this new day. Thank you for life, health, strength and soundness of mind. Order my steps and orchestrate my activities and assignments. Use me for Your glory. I thank you for peace, productivity and favor in this day that is free of confusion, frustration, distraction and all demonic interference. Thank you for Your hand of protection over our lives. Bless, save, heal, comfort and provide for my family and FB friends. Thank you for Your mercy, grace, love and forgiveness. In Jesus' mighty name I pray. Amen.

Posted on Facebook January 25, 2013

Dear Heavenly Father, thank you for this day that You have made. I will rejoice and be glad in it. It's already the last Friday of the month. Help me to be diligent and finish strong. I decree and declare peace, order, productivity and favor over this day and weekend. I come against confusion, frustration, distraction, accident, and all satanic attack and demonic interference. Thank you for health, strength and soundness of mind. Thank you for mercy, grace, love and forgiveness. Bless, save, heal, comfort and provide for my family and FB friends in need right now. May they seek You, trust You, surrender to You. God, You're faithful, and I love and trust You. Thank you, Lord. In Jesus' mighty name. Amen. Happy Friday!!!!!

Posted on Facebook January 26, 2013

Dear Heavenly Father, thank you for another day! Energize me for all that must be done today. I thank you that my family is blessed, our future is blessed, our fitness is blessed, and our finances are blessed. I thank you that no weapon formed against us shall prosper. I thank you for protection, provision, preservation, promotion, favor and peace. I plead the blood of Jesus over every family member and declare every member shall fulfill Your assignment for our lives. Move in the lives of my FB friends to save, heal, comfort, restore and deliver. Thank you, Lord. I love, honor and adore You. In Jesus' mighty and matchless name. Amen. Have a safe and wonderful weekend!

Posted on Facebook January 28, 2013

Dear Heavenly Father, thank you, Lord, for this new day that You have made. Thank you for the excellent teaching and equipping received yesterday. I praise, honor and adore You. There is no one like You. You are worthy of all my praise. Order my steps. Use me for Your glory and demonstrate Your power through me. Bless, save, heal, comfort, encourage, deliver and provide for those in need. Thank you, Lord! In Jesus' name. Amen.

Posted on Facebook January 30, 2013

Father God, thank you for satisfying my parents with 45 wonderful, blessed years of marriage. I pray that You continue to keep them in good health, strength, and soundness of mind. I am THANKFUL for their love, guidance and example. In Jesus' name, amen

Posted on Facebook January 30, 2013

Dear Heavenly Father, I lift up my family, friends, and acquaintances to You. I pray for salvation for those who don't know You in the pardoning of their sins. I pray for healing for those going through physical, mental or emotional challenges. I pray for comfort for those experiencing the loss of a loved one or relationship. I pray for provision for those in need. God, You are faithful. Thank you, Lord. In Jesus' name. Amen.

Posted on Facebook January 31, 2013

More than 40 people have been shot dead in Chicago since the beginning of the year. There were 506 homicides in the city last year. The madness has got to stop. Father God, I pray for comfort and strength for the family and friends of Hadiya Pendleton. Surround them with Your love and peace. Meet their needs as a result of this sudden loss. I plead the blood of Jesus over Chicago. Arrest every demonic spirit influencing the violence. Have mercy Lord. In Jesus' name, amen.

Posted on Facebook February 2, 2013

This is the day The Lord has made. Thank you, Father God for life, health, breath, strength, wholeness and soundness of mind. Order my steps and orchestrate my day. Thank you for peace and productivity in this day. Thank you that confusion and frustration are far from me. Thank you for protection throughout this day and weekend. Be glorified in my life and use me to be a blessing. Heal, save, comfort and provide for those in need. Lord, I love, honor and adore You. In Jesus' name. Amen

Posted on Facebook February 4, 2013

Dear Heavenly Father, thank you for this new day! Order my steps and orchestrate the events and activities concerning me. I thank you for peace, productivity, protection and favor in this day over my family and I. Bless, save, heal, comfort, encourage, protect, deliver and provide for those in need. Thank you for blessing my fitness, family, finances and future. Thank you for supernatural reset. In Jesus' name. Amen.

Posted on Facebook February 6, 2013

Dear Heavenly Father, I thank you for this day that You have made. I thank you for mercy, grace and forgiveness. I thank you that no weapon formed against me, my family, my future, my fitness or my purpose shall prosper. I thank you for peace, protection, provision, promotion and favor. Use me for Your glory. Bless, save, heal, deliver, comfort, encourage and provide for my family and FB friends and their family members and friends. Demonstrate Your power, Lord. In Jesus' name. Amen.

Posted on Facebook February 7, 2013

Dear God, please give me sweet sleep and rest. May these 5 hours feel like 10 when I wake. May I be refreshed and restored and ready for the day ahead. Thank you, Lord, for a productive night. In Jesus' name. Amen.

Posted on Facebook February 9, 2013

Father God, thank you for this new day. Thank you for diversion sin life that bring about Your perfect plan. Order my steps, orchestrate my days and use me for Your glory. Bless, save, heal, comfort and provide for those in need. Protect and keep safe those in the northeast being impacted by the winter storms. I decree and declare peace, productivity and favor over this day and weekend. I love You and thank You, Lord. In Jesus' name. Amen. Have a wonderful weekend family and FB friends!

Posted on Facebook February 12, 2013

Dear Heavenly Father, thank you for this new day. Thank you for the best life from a relationship with Your Son Jesus enjoying Your promises: forgiveness, continual presence, hope, peace, and a forever future in His presence. Bless, heal, save, comfort and provide for those in need. Thank you, Lord. In Jesus' name. Amen.

Posted on Facebook February 14, 2013

Dear Heavenly Father, thank you for this excellent day! As I begin my travel to the East coast, I pray for traveling mercies by bus, plane, and automobile both going and coming. I pray for peace, order, productivity and favor throughout this entire weekend. I come against delays, breakdowns, malfunctions, distractions and all demonic interference. I even pray for a pleasant and peaceful check-in experience and flight. Keep me focused and may my attitude and actions reflect the light of Christ. I thank you for protection over my family. Demonstrate Your power in and through me. Thank you for health, strength and soundness of mind. I love You and Thank You, Lord. In Jesus' name. Amen. MSU here I come.

Posted on Facebook February 15, 2013

Dear Heavenly Father, I pray for safe travels for all schools and volunteers making their way to ASU, MSU, NCAT, PVA&M and TSU this weekend. I pray for an excellent tournament in every location. I pray for sweet sleep tonight. May we be rested, refreshed and ready for the day ahead. Thank you, Lord, for this productive day. In Jesus' name. Amen.

Posted on Facebook February 17, 2013

Father God, thank you for a good weekend. Getting to have dinner with family was great. Give us pleasant and safe travels back to LAX and our homes. I pray for favor throughout this Supernatural day, Thank you, Lord. In Jesus. Amen.

Posted on Facebook February 23, 2013

Father God, thank you for this wonderful and productive day. Help me to accomplish much in the next few waking hours. Lord, I lift up my family, friends, church family and acquaintances to You and pray for physical, mental, emotional, relational, marital and financial healing and breakthrough. Demonstrate Your power in the lives of Your people. Give wisdom, direction, and clarity. Touch hearts and minds. Comfort, strengthen and encourage those in need. Provide peace, protection, provision and hope for those crying out to You. Father, You are faithful and more than able. I plead the blood of Jesus over that one who can't see a way out and think ending their life is the only option. Arrest tormenting spirits now. Thank you God! In Jesus' mighty and matchless name I pray. Amen.

Posted on Facebook February 24, 2013

Father God, I thank you for this powerful, impactful day and night of worship, word and ministry. Order my steps and orchestrate my life. I embrace Your plan and purpose for my life. Give me wisdom and discernment. I pray for discipline and self-control in every area. Be glorified in my life and bless me to be a blessing. In Jesus' name. Amen.

Posted on Facebook February 25, 2013

Dear Heavenly Father, thank you for this new day and week. Thank you for discipline and self-control. Thank you for peace, provision, protection and preservation. Thank you for wisdom and direction. Thank you for insight and discernment. Thank you for victory and favor in every area. Demonstrate Your power in the lives of Your people. Bless my Pastors and church family. Thank you for preparing us to possess the promise. You are faithful, and I trust You! In Jesus' name. Amen.

Posted on Facebook February 25, 2013

Father God, thank you for this productive day and peaceful evening. Rest me over the next few hours and may I be rested and refreshed when I wake for a super early work day. Thank you for protection, provision and preservation. Thank you for health, strength, and soundness of mind. My family, fitness, finances and future are blessed. You are faithful, and I thank and trust You. In Jesus' name. Amen.

Posted on Facebook February 27, 2013

Dear Heavenly Father, thank you, Lord, for this new day. Thank you for mercy and grace. Thank you for love and forgiveness. Bless, save, heal, comfort, encourage, deliver, restore and provide for those in need. Demonstrate Your power. Use me for Your glory. Thank you for this season. In Jesus' name. Amen.

Posted on Facebook March 2, 2013

Thank you, Lord, for this new day! Have a great day all! Father God ,I pray for traveling mercies for my niece and friend safely to California. Surround them with favor throughout. Keep every mode of transportation safe and may the flight be peaceful. Thank you, Lord. In Jesus' name. Amen.

Posted on Facebook March 4, 2013

Dear Heavenly Father, thank you for this new day, week and month. Thank you for the supernatural changes that have already taken place and will take place. Thank you for wisdom, understanding, and discernment. Thank you Holy Spirit for guidance and direction. I decree and declare peace, order, productivity and favor over this day, week and month. Thank you that my family, fitness, finances and future are all blessed. Thank you for protection, provision and promotion. Bless, heal, save, deliver, comfort, encourage and provide for those in need. Thank you, Lord. In Jesus' mighty name. Amen.

Dear Heavenly Father, thank you for this new day. Thank you, God for your faithfulness, mercy and grace. Thankful that You have the final word. We choose to believe Your report. I lift up everyone in need of healing, comfort, strength, encouragement, salvation, deliverance, guidance, joy, peace, provision and pardon. Demonstrate Your power in the lives of Your people. Thank you, Lord! In Jesus' name, amen. Trust Him , y'all!

Father God, thank you for this new day. Thank you for health, strength and soundness of mind. Bless the singles conference this weekend and all facilitators, attendees, and workers. Order my steps this day. I thank you for peace, productivity and favor in this day. I thank you that frustration and confusion are far from me. I thank you that my family, fitness, finances and future are all blessed. You are faithful, and I love and trust You. In Jesus' name. Amen. Happy Friday y'all!

Father God, I thank you for this new day. I pray for traveling grace and favor as my nieces return to MD. Get them to LAX safely and on time. I come against frustration and confusion. I pray for peace over their entire day. Thank you, Lord. In Jesus' name. Amen.

Father God, I praise You, Lord. I honor and adore You. You are great and greatly to be praised. This is the day that You have made. I am glad and will rejoice in it. I decree and declare peace, order, productivity and favor over this day. I come against confusion, frustration, distractions and all satanic attack and demonic influences. I thank you for souls saves, lives changed, and hearts encouraged this day. I thank you for relationships restored and bodies healed. Demonstrate your power this day. I pray for supernatural strength in our bodies to carry out every assignment today. You, God, are so faithful. Thank you, Lord. In Jesus' mighty name. Amen!

Dear Heavenly Father, thank you for this new day. Thank you in advance that it is peaceful, productive, fruitful and favor-filled. Use me for Your glory. In Jesus' mighty name. Amen. Have a blessed day!

Dear Heavenly Father, thank you for this new day that You have made. Thank you for grace to complete every God-ordained assignment. During this health improvement process show me who and what needs to be released that I may be in Your perfect will. I lift up those in need of supernatural healing in their bodies and their family members in need of strength to walk them through. I lift up those in need of comfort and peace that passes understanding who have lost loved ones. Demonstrate your power Jehovah God. I thank you for peace, order and productivity in this day. I praise, honor and adore You, Father. In Jesus' mighty name. Amen. Happy Monday!

This is the Best day The Lord has made. I am grateful and so glad in it. Dear Heavenly Father, thank you for another year of life. Thank you for Your continued faithfulness. Order my steps this day and year and orchestrate the activities and assignments of my life. Demonstrate Your power through me and use me for Your glory. Thank you for growth in every area. Thank you for wisdom, discernment and discretion. Thank you for discipline and self-control. Thank you for satisfying me with long life and showing me Your salvation. My best is yet to come, and I trust You. My fitness, family, finances and future are blessed. Thank you for peace, productivity, favor, and fruitfulness on my life. Thank you for protection and provision. Bless, heal, save, comfort, deliver and provide for those in need. Thank you, Lord. I love, honor and adore You. There is no one like You, no one greater than You. In Jesus' mighty and matchless name I pray. Amen. Have a blessed day all!

Father God, You, are my Source. I thank you for provision. You are my Shepherd, and I shall not want for all my needs are met. Lead and guide me where You want me to go. In You God I live, move and have my being. I thank you that my family, fitness, finances and future are blessed, and You satisfy us with long life and show us Your salvation. Touch those in need of salvation, healing, comfort, peace, strength, deliverance, protection, provision and restoration. Thank you, Lord. In Jesus' mighty name. Amen! Have a blessed day family and FB friends!

Father God, I lift up Aria's (a straight-A teen who died after inhaling computer cleaner amid huffing trend) family, friends, and classmates and pray for comfort and encouragement for them. Surround them with peace and strengthen them in their time of loss. Meet all their needs. I pray a hedge of protection over the minds of our teenagers from temptation and lies of the enemy. I pray against inhalant abuse and come against premature death. Heal like only You can, Lord. In Jesus' name, amen. Pray and cover our children.

Father God, thank you for this new day that You have made. Order our steps and orchestrate the activities of this day and weekend from start to finish. I lift up the eighth graders and advisors of Holmes Middle school and Porter Middle school as they travel to Baltimore/DC. I pray for traveling mercies both in the air and on the ground. I pray for favor and safety over the entire group. I pray for protection from accident and injury. I pray for cooperation with and respect of one another. May it be a fun and exciting time of learning as they visit all the sites on tour. Thank you, Lord. In Jesus' name. Amen.

Dear Heavenly Father, thank you for this new day. We celebrate You as King of Kings and Lord of Lords. I lift up my Pastors and church family to You right now. I pray a hedge of protection around every member and their family. I plead the blood of Jesus over every member. I pray for quick and complete healing. I pray for strength and encouragement. I prayer for focus, favor and the will to fight knowing the battle is already won. I thank you, Lord, that we already have the victory through You. Demonstrate Your power, Jehovah God, in the lives of Your people. We will possess the promise. We will not back down. The enemy is defeated, and we will fulfill Your perfect plan for our lives. Touch our Senior Pastors, our Pastoral team, and every leader and worker. We thank you for miracles, signs and wonders. We thank you that your Word is taught this day with boldness as You give utterance. We thank you that hearts are open to receive, souls are saved, hearts are encouraged, and lives are forever changed. Anoint every vessel who will minister/serve today at Living Praise Christian Center Lancaster and Chatsworth. In Jesus' mighty name I pray. Amen.

Father God which art in Heaven, hallowed be thy name. Thank you for this new day. Thank you for mercy, grace, love and forgiveness. Thank you for never leaving us nor forsaking us. Thank you for wisdom, knowledge and discernment for every relationship and assignment. Help us to be and do what You called us to do. Lord, I lift up my family, FB friends, church family, and their family members. Heal minds and bodies that need a supernatural touch from You. Nothing is impossible with You. Demonstrate Your power in the lives of Your people. Comfort and encourage those experiencing the loss of a loved one or relationship. I pray for provision for those in need of a breakthrough. I pray for rededication for all who walked away from You for whatever reason. Speak peace to them right now. Invade their darkness with Your light. Forgive our sins and heal our land, God. Thank you, Lord. In Jesus' name. Amen. To God be all glory and honor!

Posted on Facebook March 27, 2013

Father God, thank you for Your mercy, grace, love, forgiveness and correction. I am determined and dedicated to being physically, spiritually, mentally, emotionally, relationally and financially fit in 2013. I can do all things through Christ who gives me strength. Help me, Lord, to be who You've called me to be. You are faithful, and I trust You! In Jesus' mighty name. Amen.

Posted on Facebook March 28, 2013

The street with the home where the young girl was kidnapped from yesterday is still blocked with a police presence. Father God, arrest the kidnappers and give them no rest/peace until they surrender and confess all. Heal this girl's mind, body and emotions. Touch her family as well and give them peace in their home. Thank you, Lord. In Jesus' name. Amen.

Posted on Facebook March 29, 2013

Dear Heavenly Father, I come, in the name of Jesus, thanking You for this new day. I celebrate this Good Friday because Your Son got up with all power in His hands, on Resurrection Sunday. Jesus died for me, so I shall live for Him to the Glory of God. I pray that in services, plays, and programs across the nation and the world that You would be glorified, souls would be saved, hearts healed and lives forever changed. Demonstrate Your saving, healing, life-changing, miraculous power this day and weekend. Thank you, Lord, for peace, productivity, provision and protection this day and weekend. No weapon formed against my family or purpose shall prosper. I walk in victory for the enemy is defeated. Bless, heal, save, comfort, deliver, rescue and redeem those in need right now. God, You are faithful! Order my steps and orchestrate my activities. Use me for Your glory. Thank you, Lord. In Jesus' mighty and matchless name. Amen. Happy and Blessed Good Friday!

Posted on Facebook March 31, 2013

Happy and Blessed Resurrection Sunday family and FB friends! Because He lives, we can have eternal life. Time to prepare for worship. Father

God, demonstrate Your power today – save souls, heal hearts, restore relationships, touch bodies and minds. You are the One True and Faithful God! Thank you, Lord! In Jesus' name. Amen!

Posted on Facebook April 3, 2013

Dear Heavenly Father, thank you for this new day that You have made. Thank you for health, healing and wholeness. I pray for protection and safe travels as staff and volunteers make our way to Torrance for the 2013 HCASC NCT as well as for teams and Presidents. I pray for peace, order, productivity, protection and favor over this event. I come against confusion, frustration, injury, accidents and all demonic interference. Bless, heal, protect, comfort, strengthen, encourage, deliver and provide for my family, church family and FB friends. God, You are so faithful and I thank you! Demonstrate Your power this day and use me for Your glory. In Jesus' name. Amen!

Posted on Facebook April 7, 2013

Another night to sleep fast. Work day done. Dear God, please multiply these four hours and let them feel like eight. May I rest sound and wake rested and refreshed. Thank you, Lord. In Jesus' name. Amen

Posted on Facebook April 9, 2013

This has been a great but long seven days. Will be asleep before midnight tonight. Dear Heavenly Father, I pray for safe and timely travel for every team and volunteer returning home from HCASC NCT on Wednesday. I pray for no equipment malfunction, no delays, no inclement weather and no other setbacks that would damper their day. Thank you, Lord. In Jesus' name. Amen.

Posted on Facebook April 12, 2013

Father God ,thank you for this new day. Thank you, Lord, for health, strength and soundness of mind. Thank you for protection and provision. I thank you for peace, order and productivity in this day. I thank you that confusion and frustration are far from me. Thank you for wisdom, understanding, discernment and favor in every area of life. Bless, heal, save, comfort, strengthen, deliver, restore and provide for my family, pastors, church family and friends. Use me for Your glory. Thank you, Lord! In Jesus' name. Amen. Happy Friday!

Posted on Facebook April 19, 2013

Dear Heavenly Father, thank you for this day that You have made. Hear from heaven, forgive our sin and heal our land. I pray that we will humble ourselves, pray, seek Your face and turn from our wicked ways. God, comfort the grieving, heal the sick, strengthen the weak, calm the confused, provide for those in need. I pray for godly counsel and wisdom to guide the decisions of those in authority. I thank you for peace, provision and protection. I thank you that no weapon formed against my purpose and destiny shall prosper. Demonstrate Your power, Lord, this day. In Jesus' name with thanksgiving, I pray, amen. Happy Friday family and FB friends!

Posted on Facebook April 20, 2013

Father God, I thank you for the victory that is ours in Christ Jesus. I lift up my family members, church family, and FB friends to You right now. I pray for comfort for those experiencing the loss of a loved one. I pray for healing for those experiencing challenges in their body. I pray for peace, mental strength and encouragement for those tormented, depressed or discouraged. I pray for provision for those experiencing lack. I pray for salvation for all who do not know You in the pardoning of their sins. Deliver and set free. Give us sweet sleep. Protect us as we slumber and those who may work the night shift. You are faithful, and I thank you. In Jesus' name. Amen.

Posted on Facebook April 22, 2013

Father God, when we hurt You feel our hurt. I lift up everyone that is feeling discouraged. Restore, refresh and renew them. Comfort those missing a child, parent, a spouse or other loved one due to death last night, last month, last year or several years ago. I come against guilt and regret. I pray for peace for those in the midst of decision-making.

Heal like only You can, Lord. Thank you for hearing and answering. In Jesus' name. Amen.

Dear Heavenly Father, we thank you for this day that You have made, and we rejoice in it. We thank you for brand new mercies. Great is Your faithfulness. We decree and declare peace, order ,productivity and favor over our day. We thank you that everyone and everything including ourselves cooperate with Your perfect will for our lives. We thank you for Divine connections and assignments this day. We thank you for discernment to know what or who may be a distraction. We pray for salvation for our unsaved loved ones. We pray for healing for those with physical, mental or emotional challenges. We pray for provision for those in need. We pray for comfort, strength and encouragement for the hurting, grieving or discouraged. Demonstrate Your power this day. Father God, only You are worthy of our praise, honor, and glory. We love, adore and worship You this day. We thank you, Lord, for hearing and answering. In Jesus' mighty name. Amen.

Father God, thank you for this dynamic day of wonderful worship, powerful preaching, excellent learning, and a fun family time. Souls were saved, lives changed, hearts encouraged, and chains were broken. God, You are amazing. Rest us tonight and wake us refreshed and ready for the day. As we finish April and enter May, I lift up my family members, pastors, church family and FB friends to You. I pray for blessings, healing, salvation, recovery deliverance, comfort, strength, encouragement, protection, provision and peace. God, demonstrate Your power in the lives of Your people this week. Thank you, Lord, for hearing and answering. In Jesus' name, amen. Goodnight and God bless.

This is the day The Lord has made. I will rejoice and be glad in it. Father God, thank you for another chance to say thank you. Thank you for health, strength and soundness of mind. Thank you for protection, provision and peace. Thank you for forgiveness and favor. Thank you for mercy and grace. Thank you for satisfying me and my family members with long, healthy, abundant life and showing us Your salvation. Thank you for never leaving us nor forsaking us. Bless, save, heal, comfort, deliver, encourage and provide for all who will receive Your precious gifts. Touch hearts and minds. Invade darkness with Your light. Pour out Your peace where there is confusion. Bring joy where hope is gone. Use me for Your glory this day. You are faithful, and I love and trust You. In Jesus' mighty name, amen. Have a God-blessed, God-directed day!

Posted on Facebook May 2, 2013

Dear Heavenly Father, I lift up everyone traveling to graduation ceremonies and celebrations this week and month for their loved ones. I pray for protection on land and in the air. I thank you for safe arrival today for Dad and I. I thank you for pleasant, peaceful and favor-filled flights going and returning. I pray for protection over our family members and homes. I lift up graduates everywhere and pray that celebrations won't turn into tragedy. Thank you, Lord! In Jesus' name. Amen.

Posted on Facebook May 2, 2013

Dear Heavenly Father, thank you for a new day. On this day where we pause as a country to realize the importance of prayer, I pray for lasting change. Your Word declares, "Blessed is the nation whose God is The Lord." I pray that the United States of America return to You for direction and guidance. You've given us free will so we must choose. I pray for peace, protection, and provision in our land. I pray for healing, salvation and revival in our land. Thank you for mercy, grace and forgiveness. I love, honor and adore You! You are the only true and living God. Demonstrate Your power in the lives of Your people. In Your Son's name Jesus, I pray, amen.

Posted on Facebook May 6, 2013

Dear Heavenly Father, thank you for this day that You have made. Thank you for health, strength and soundness of mind. Thank you for never leaving us or forsaking us. Thank you for peace, order, productivity, protection and favor this day. Thank you that confusion, frustration and distraction are far from me. Thank you for victory in every area. Bless, heal, save, comfort, encourage, strengthen, deliver, provide for my family members and friends. Show Yourself strong on behalf of Your people. Demonstrate Your power on behalf of LPCC this day. I thank you, Lord, that my fitness, finances, family and future are all blessed. Use me for Your glory. Thank you, Lord! In Jesus' name, amen.

Posted on Facebook May 10, 2013

Father God, I thank you for Your faithfulness and forgiveness. I thank you for Your love, care and compassion. I thank you for Your mercy and grace. Bless, heal, save, comfort, strengthen, encourage, deliver and provide for my family and friends. Minister to the needs of Your people. Demonstrate Your power in their lives. Show Yourself strong on their behalf. Use me for Your glory this day. Order my steps. Thank you, Lord! In Jesus' name. Amen!

Posted on Facebook May 12, 2013

Father God, I lift up this family to You right now and pray that their loved one shall not die but live to declare Your mighty works. Demonstrate Your healing power! Thank you, Lord, for peace and favor in every arrangement that needs to be made. Thank you, Lord, for hearing and answering. In Jesus' mighty name. Amen.

Posted on Facebook May 17, 2013

Dear Heavenly Father, You are so faithful. Thank you for bringing us to Friday. Thank you for health, strength and soundness of mind. I pray for peace, order, protection and favor over this day and weekend. Order our steps and orchestrate our activities. Bless, save, heal, comfort and provide for my family and FB friends. Demonstrate Your power in the lives of Your people. Heal us to help others. Thank you, Lord. In Jesus' name. Amen.

Posted on Facebook May 20, 2013

Dear Heavenly Father, we lift up Oklahoma to You and all impacted either directly or indirectly by today's tornado. Comfort the grieving, heal the injured and strengthen the survivors. Bless and encourage the first responders and all those helping with the recovery efforts. I pray for more people to be found alive. Demonstrate Your power, God. You are still faithful. Thank you, Lord. In Jesus' name, amen.

Posted on Facebook May 24, 2013

Dear Heavenly Father, thank you for this day that You have made. I rejoice and am grateful and glad in it. I lift up my family and friends and pray that You bless, save, heal, comfort, strengthen, encourage, deliver and provide for those in need. I decree and declare peace, order and productivity over this day and come against confusion, frustration and distractions. Thank you for Your continued protection. Order my steps and use me for Your glory. You are faithful, and I trust You. In Jesus' mighty name. Amen!

Posted on Facebook May 28, 2013

Dear Heavenly Father, thank you for this new day that You have made. Thank you for the wake-up call. Thank you for health, strength and soundness of mind. Thank you for protection and provision. Thank you for peace, order, and productivity over this day. Thank you for mercy and grace. Order my steps and use me to be a blessing. Thank you for salvation and security, forgiveness and favor. Thank you for wisdom and discernment. Demonstrate Your power this day. Heal, save, comfort and deliver those in need. Restore relationships. God, You are great! You are faithful! You can be trusted. Thank you for loving me. In Jesus' name. Amen.

Posted on Facebook May 31, 2013

Dear Heavenly Father, thank you for this new day that You have made. You are faithful and can be trusted. Thank you for protection and provision. Thank you for health and healing. Thank you for care and compassion. Thank you for salvation and eternal security. Bless those in need of peace, comfort, salvation, strength, encouragement, healing, protection and provision. Demonstrate Your power this day. Order every step and orchestrate every activity. You are faithful, and I trust You. Thank you, Lord. In Jesus' name. Amen. Happy Friday! Be safe.

Posted on Facebook June 2, 2013

Father God, thank you for Your mercy, grace, love, care, compassion and forgiveness. Thank you for correction and direction. Help me to be who and what You've called me to be. I can through Christ who strengthens me. Thank you, Lord! In Jesus' name. Amen. Have a safe and blessed day!

Posted on Facebook June 2, 2013

As my journey to Onederland and a physically, spiritually, mentally, emotionally and financially healthier me continues, it's time to focus more in certain areas. It's a new season and a new day. Father God, thank you for growth, increase, elevation and promotion. Thank you for miracles, signs and wonders. Thank you that my fitness, family, finances and future are all blessed! Thank you for wisdom and discernment. Thank you, Lord! In Jesus' name. Amen. I'm signing off for a season.

Posted on Facebook June 23, 2013

The owner of Wallace Daycare Center has gone to her eternal home. Father God, I thank you for the life of my grandmother and for satisfying her with 93 years. She outlived her husband by 20 years and was the last of her siblings. She was ready to go so, as we prepare to celebrate her life, bless, comfort and encourage our family. I pray for safe travels. I pray for peace, order, and productivity throughout this time of preparation. I pray for favor. I pray for healing in every area. I pray we all get adequate rest and for supernatural strength for what is needed. I even pray for nice, sunny weather for the service and burial. I come against confusion, frustration and the slightest irritation. Use me for Your glory. Demonstrate Your healing, saving, restoring power in our lives. Meet every need. Thank you, Lord, for my family. Bless, heal, save, comfort, strengthen, deliver and provide for all those in need. Thank you, Lord, for your continued faithfulness! In Jesus' mighty name I pray. Amen.

Posted on Facebook July 9, 2013

Dear Heavenly Father, thank you for this new day that You have made. Thank you for breath, health and soundness of mind. Thank you for mercy and grace, forgiveness and favor. Thank you for peace, protection, provision and promotion. Thank you for conviction and correction. Help me to be more like You, reflecting Your Son Jesus. I pray for salvation, healing, comfort, deliverance and strength, for those in need. Bless those calling on You in faith. Demonstrate Your power in my family, fitness, finances, on my job, and through my ministry and business. You are faithful, and I trust You. Bless my Pastors and church family. There is no one like You. No one greater than You. Heal our land, Lord. Guide us this day. Thank you, Lord. In Jesus' name. Amen.

Posted on Facebook July 21, 2013

Father God, thank you for this new day. Thank you for rich word and powerful ministry. Thank you for choosing me. Use me for Your glory. I am in expectation and great anticipation for Your presence to be manifested this week in a mighty way. Touch, save, heal, deliver, comfort, strengthen, encourage, protect, promote, elevate, rebuild, renovate, restore and provide for all in need. You are faithful, and I trust You. Thank you, Abba! In Jesus' mighty name. Amen.

Posted on Facebook July 23, 2013

Father God, thank you for this new breaking of day. Thank you for breath, health, strength, wholeness and soundness of mind. God, there is no one like You, no one greater than You. I pray for peace, order, productivity and favor in our lives. I pray for healing of hearts, minds and bodies. I pray for salvation of souls and restoration of relationships. Heal our land, heal our country, heal this nation. I pray for revival and return to Godly, Biblical principles. You are the Only firm foundation. Have mercy on us Lord. Thank you for loving us enough to send Jesus. I praise, honor and adore You. In Jesus' mighty name. Amen.

Posted on Facebook July 27, 2013

Father God, thank you for this day that You have made. I pray for strength and protection throughout this day. Be glorified in our lives. Bless my family, FB friends, Pastors and church family. Heal, comfort, save, encourage, deliver and provide for all in need. Thank you for this new season. In Jesus' name. Amen! Have a wonderful weekend all!

Posted on Facebook July 31, 2013

Father God, thank you for this new day! I pray for peace, order, productivity and favor in this day. I thank you for 3 wonderful, blessed years of marriage. God, You, are faithful! I lift up my family and friends and pray for salvation, healing, deliverance, protection, provision, comfort, strength, encouragement and peace of mind. You know their need. Demonstrate Your power. All glory and honor belongs to You. In Jesus' mighty name. Amen.

Posted on Facebook August 2, 2013

Father God, thank you for this day that You have made. Thank you for new beginnings, new favor, new openings, new opportunities. Thank you for manifestation of promises. Thank you for answered prayers. Thank you for loved one's salvation. Thank you for physical, mental, emotional, marital, relational and spiritual healing. Thank you for protection, promotion and provision. Thank you for successful surgeries. Thank you for supernatural strength and peace through the grief process. Thank you for grace for every assignment. Thank you for restoration of relationships. Thank you, God for victory in every area. Thank you for release and increase. Thank you for renewed minds and transformed lives for the participants at Space of Grace Youth conference. Thank you for safe travels going and coming. Thank you for blessing me to be a blessing. Thank you for never leaving me or forsaking me. Be glorified in and through my life. In Jesus' name. Amen.

Posted on Facebook August 5, 2013

Father God, thank you for this new day. Thank you for the opportunity to share Your love and shine Your light. Thank you for salvation and eternal security through Your Son Jesus. Thank you for protection, provision, promotion and most importantly peace. Thank you for favor in every area and blessed fitness, finances and family members. I pray that You provide healing, strength, comfort, salvation, encouragement, provision and protection for those in need right now. God, You are faithful, and I trust You. Thank you for health, healing and wholeness. Order my steps and orchestrate my day. Thank you Holy Spirit for guiding and leading me. Thank you Lord for loving me. I praise, honor and adore You. In Jesus' mighty name. Amen. Happy Blessed Monday all!

Posted on Facebook August 5, 2013

Father God, I lift up the victims involved in the amber alert just issued. I pray for a safe ending. Reveal the whereabouts of that vehicle to the proper authorities. Bring conviction to the suspects. Thank you, Lord. In Jesus' name. Amen.

Posted on Facebook August 9, 2013

Father God which art in Heaven hallowed be Your name. Thank you for this new day that You have made. Thank you for sweet sleep. I pray for peace and strength for those who couldn't sleep. May they cast every care on You. I thank you for breath, health and soundness of mind. I pray for those in need of physical, mental and emotional healing. I pray for accurate diagnosis and treatment. I pray for torment and confusion to cease. I pray for bodies, minds and hearts to be made whole. I thank you for provision for every need and overflow to bless others. I pray for those in need of food, clothes, and shelter. Approve that rental application with low to no security deposit. Send help to those who can't see a way out. You are faithful. I thank you for salvation and eternal security. I pray for those who never knew You, who walked away from You or who rejected You. May their hearts be open to receive Your life-changing gift through Your Son Jesus. I praise, honor and adore You. Thank you for mercy, grace and forgiveness. I pray for those in prison because they won't forgive others or themselves. May they receive Your love that makes it possible. Demonstrate Your power this day. In Jesus' name. Amen.

Posted on Facebook August 9, 2013

Guy next to me on the elliptical announced to his friends in the course of their conversation that he is atheist. Get him, God. Father God, You wish that none perish. I lift up that young man to You right now and pray for a life-changing, soul-saving encounter with Your Son Jesus before he closes his eyes into eternity. Thank you, Lord. In Jesus' name. Amen.

Posted on Facebook August 12, 2013

Father God, thank you for this new day that You have made. As our children return to school this week, we lift them up to You. We pray for protection and plead the blood of Jesus over them from the crown of their head to the soles of their feet. We pray for favor with the administration, teachers and fellow students. We pray for focus, diligence and a productive school year. We pray for order and peace in the classroom, on the playground, physical education facilities and wherever our children must go. I come against frustration, confusion and satanic attacks. I pray for provision for those in need of school supplies, clothes, and even stability. I come against abduction, offense and premature death. I come against sickness and disease. I pray for God-ordained relationships and interactions and bind their minds to the mind of Christ. I pray for comprehension and clarity. I pray for boldness to walk in obedience to Your will. Thank you, Lord for an excellent school year. In Jesus' name. Amen.

Posted on Facebook August 19, 2013

Dear Heavenly Father, thank you for this new day. I pray for safe travels in the down pours across SoCal. I thank you for Your promises of peace, protection and provision. I pray for a productive, favor-filled day and week in our workplaces and for our children in school. May my attitude and actions be pleasing to You. Bless, save, heal, comfort, strengthen, encourage and provide for those in need. You are worthy of all the glory, honor and praise and I thank you. In Jesus' name. Amen. Happy Blessed Monday!!!

Posted on Facebook August 21, 2013

Dear Heavenly Father, I thank you for this new day. Thank you for forgiveness, mercy and grace. I lift up every member that is offended, discouraged, and frustrated in the Body of Christ and pray for healing, reconciliation and restoration. I pray for a return to their set place and appointed assignment. I pray for hearts to be healed and lives to be changed. I come against misunderstanding. I pray for revival. I pray for Your people to humble ourselves, pray, seek Your face and turn from our wicked ways. I thank you that You promise to hear from heaven, forgive our sin and heal our land. God be glorified this day.

Dear God, I lift up those in need right now. Heal, save, deliver, comfort, encourage and provide for them. I thank you for your promises of peace, protection and provision. All Your promises are yes and amen. Minister peace to that one who just lost a loved one. Cover that one who just received a negative report. Heal every hurt.

This is the day that You have made, and I rejoice and am glad in it. I decree and declare peace, order, productivity and favor over this day. You are not the author of confusion or destruction. I plead the blood of Jesus over our homes, schools, families and workplaces. I thank you for protection from the enemy and his evil devises. I pray a hedge of protection over our loved ones.

God, You are faithful and can be trusted. I thank you that You cause all things to work for my good and Your glory. Demonstrate Your power this day. Thank you, Lord. In Jesus' mighty and matchless name I pray. Amen!!!

Posted on Facebook August 26, 2013

Father God, I lift up President David Wilson, the Board of Regents, Administration, Faculty, Staff, Students and Alumni of Morgan State. I pray for wisdom in decision-making and unity and integrity. I pray for stability for continued growth. I pray for success in every area. Uncover anything and anyone with a hidden agenda contrary to the established mission of the University and set it in order. Demonstrate your power over that entire Northeast Baltimore community. Give Morgan State favor with the State of Maryland, Federal Government and private corporations that would support its success. I pray a hedge of protection around the campus that would keep evil influences away. Thank you, Lord. In Jesus' mighty name. Amen.

Posted on Facebook September 6, 2013

Father God, when I finally make it home, and to my bed, please give me sound, sweet sleep. May the few hours I get refresh and restore me for the super early day ahead of me. I pray this for Pastors and LPCC family in the same position. Thank you, Lord, for a super successful, productive ministry morning. In Jesus' name. Amen.

Posted on Facebook September 11, 2013

Dear Heavenly Father, thank you for this new day. Thank you for protection, provision and preservation. I pray for peace and productivity over this day. As we remember, may we never forget Your love for us. May we never forget Your sacrifice in the shed blood of Your Son Jesus for our salvation and eternal security. May we never forget You're our Strong Tower, our Refuge from the storm, our Shepherd, our Hiding Place, our Righteousness, our Healer, our Provider, our Constant Help. May we never forget You're a loving, forgiving God.

Father God, heal hearts and minds. Change lives and restore relationships. I pray for wisdom and understanding, for discernment, confidence and courage. Speak to me and through me.

Thank you for this new day and new season. Thank you for elevation in every area. Thank you for answered prayers. Thank you for salvation of loved ones.

Bless, save, heal, comfort, strengthen, deliver, encourage, provide for those in need and calling on You right now. Do the same for those being prayed for but don't know they need You. Demonstrate Your power this day in the lives of Your people. May we shine Your light in darkness. May we love like You love.

Heal our land. Guide our President and officials. Protect our country. You are faithful and I trust You. Thank you, Lord, for hearing and answering. In Jesus' mighty and matchless name. Amen.

Posted on Facebook September 16, 2013, 5:50 am

Dear Heavenly Father, thank you for this new day that You have made. I rejoice and am glad. Thank you for brand new mercies. Thank you for health, strength and soundness of mind. Order my steps and orchestrate my day. Give me wisdom, understanding, and discernment.

I decree and declare peace, productivity and favor over my day. I come against confusion, distractions, and all satanic attacks and demonic influences. I thank you for protection from accident or injury. I thank you for provision for every need.

I lift up my family and friends to You and pray for their needs. Heal, save, comfort, strengthen, encourage, protect, deliver, favor, and provide for those calling on You right now.

Father God, I lift up Pastors Fred and Linda Hodge, Bishop I.V. and Dr. Bridget Hilliard and the Living Praise and New Light churches and members. Demonstrate Your power. Cover Your vessels and be glorified in the services. Save souls, heal hearts and minds and change lives forever.

God, You are faithful, and can be trusted. Restore broken relationships. I call in the backslider, the hurt, the offended, the discouraged, the depressed, the confused and the deceived. Loose shackles and open prison doors.

Thank you, Lord, for hearing and answering. In Jesus' mighty and matchless name I pray. Amen.

Posted on Facebook September 16, 2013

Father God, thank you for an amazing time in Your presence. Thank you for the wisdom imparted by Bishop I.V. Hilliard tonight. Restore and Refresh him tonight and pour into him more for him to give out tomorrow. Thank you for an excellent PMT team. Bless each worker and meet every need. Give each worker sweet sleep when they lay their head down. Bless our Pastors and church family. I thank you for healing in my body and plead the blood of Jesus over this and every situation. I choose to believe the truth of Your word that says by Jesus' stripes I am healed. Guide me and give me wisdom concerning treatment. Thank you, Lord. You are faithful, and I trust You. In Jesus' name. Amen.

Posted on Facebook September 21, 2013

Father God, thank you for this new day that You have made. I am grateful and glad in it. Thank you for both forgiveness and favor. Thank you for peace, protection and provision in my life. Thank you for salvation and eternal security. Thank you for family and fellowship with believers. Thank you for purpose and destiny.

Go before me this day and keep us from danger seen and unseen. Order my steps and use me to be a blessing. May I be in tuned to the leading of the Holy Spirit to discern distractions from divine encounters. Demonstrate Your power, Lord.

Bless, heal, save, comfort, strengthen, deliver, encourage and provide for all calling on You this day. Thank you, Lord, for Your care, love and compassion. Be glorified this day. In Jesus' mighty name. Amen.

Happy Blessed Day! Excited and In Expectation... My fitness, finances, family and future are all blessed!

Posted on Facebook October 13, 2013

Father God, thank you for this day that You have made. I pray for peace, order, productivity and protection over this day. I pray for healing in hearts, minds and bodies. I pray for the word to be preached with confidence and clarity. I pray for workers in abundance serving joyfully onto The Lord on their post. I pray for souls to be saved, lives changed, and members added to the church. Be glorified. Guide us this day Holy Spirit. Thank you, Lord. In Jesus' name. Amen.

Posted on Facebook October 24, 2013

Father God, thank you for this new day that You have made. I pray for peace, productivity and protection this day. I plead the blood of Jesus over our schools, workplaces, and communities. I pray for healing in our land. Demonstrate Your power and be glorified in our lives.

Heal those with challenges in their body. Comfort those who've lost or anticipating the loss of a loved one. Deliver those caught up in depression, discouragement and deception of the enemy. Shine Your light in those dark places.

Provide for those experiencing lack. Strengthen and encourage those who think they can't make it. You are the Healer, Provider, Peace, Protector, Restorer, Redeemer. Heal hearts, minds, hurts, lives and relationships. You are the only source of real peace and joy.

Thank you, Father, for forgiveness, grace, mercy, compassion, love, favor. Thank you for never leaving or forsaking us. In Jesus' mighty name. Amen.

Posted on Facebook October 31, 2013

Father God, thank you for this new day that You have made. I plead the blood of Jesus over my family and friends and come against accident, injury and premature death. Demonstrate Your power in the lives of Your people. Thank you, Lord. In Jesus' name. Amen. Be wise and safe today people.

Posted on Facebook November 9, 2013

Father God, thank you for this new day that You have made. I pray for safe travels throughout the day. I pray for great family fellowship and fun. I pray for physical and mental strength and stamina. I pray for health and wholeness. I pray for all participants of this 5K especially those directly or indirectly impacted by cancer or domestic violence. Heal like only You can. God, You are so faithful! Thank you, Lord! In Jesus' mighty name. Amen!

Posted on Facebook November 15, 2013

Father, thank you for this new day. I rejoice. I'm grateful. I'm glad. Thank you in advance for a peaceful, super productive day. Thank you for supernatural strength. In Jesus' name. Amen. Happy Friday!!!

Posted on Facebook November 18, 2013

Father God, this is the day that You have made. I rejoice and am glad in it. Thank you for brand new mercies! Thank you for peace, protection and provision.

I pray for turnaround in the lives of my family and friends. I pray for salvation for those who don't know You, rededication for those who walked away from You, deliverance for those deceived by the enemy, healing for those going through challenges, comfort, strength and encouragement for those depressed and discouraged, provision for those experiencing lack.

God, You, are faithful and can be trusted. You wish that none perish but that all would come to repentance. I pray that each one would be receptive to an encounter with You today. Move Holy Spirit. Thank you, Abba! In Jesus' mighty name. Amen.

Posted on Facebook November 22, 2013

Father God, had grandma not passed away in June she would be 94 years young today. I lift up my family especially my mom, aunts and uncles to You and pray for comfort, strength, and encouragement. I come against depression, discouragement, and regret. I pray we all celebrate life and live it to the fullest led by Your Holy Spirit. Thank you for the time we had to share with her. I pray for all reading this post who may be remembering, experiencing or anticipating the loss of a loved one. Shower them with peace and love right now. Thank you, Abba. In Jesus' name, Amen. This is the day that the Lord has made. I will rejoice and be glad in it.

Posted on Facebook November 28, 2013

Happy Blessed Thanksgiving to my family and friends! Father God, I lift up those who are not happy right now. I pray for comfort and encouragement for those who've lost a loved one whether today, last month, last year or longer. I pray for peace and strength for those whose loved one may be transitioning from life to death. I pray for healing for those going through challenges. I pray for provision for those in need. I pray for breakthrough for the depressed or discouraged. I pray for protection and safety for all traveling this holiday weekend. Demonstrate Your power. Thank you Lord. In Jesus' mighty name. Amen. God is faithful and can be trusted.

Posted on Facebook December 2, 2013

Father God, I pray for my niece and all Morgan students as well as everyone taking finals this week. They can do all things through Christ who strengthens them. May they have balance and wisdom on when to study and when to rest. Touch, surround and protect. Thank you, Lord. In Jesus' mighty name. Amen.

Posted on Facebook December 3, 2013

Father God, I pray for the safe return of the 3 children taken by the mother in the current Amber Alert. Protect them physically and emotionally. Convict this mother to do the right thing. Thank you, Lord. In Jesus' name.

Posted on Facebook December 8, 2013

Father God, thank you for the life of Mr. Jack Dennis. He was always joking, laughing and loving life. I lift up to You Mrs. Dennis, his family and every member of the Morgan family. I pray for comfort and encouragement. Thank you, Lord. In Jesus' name. Amen.

Posted on Facebook December 13, 2013

Father God, thank you for this new day that You have made. Order my steps and use me to be a blessing.

Meet the needs of my family members and FBF calling on You right now. Heal, save, comfort, deliver, strengthen, encourage, favor and provide for, restore and rebuild.

Thank you, Lord. You are so good. Thank you for Your care and compassion, Your love and forgiveness. Demonstrate Your power this day. In Jesus' name. Amen. Happy Friday! Trust God and seek Him 1st!

Posted on Facebook December 14, 2013, 6:04 am

Father God, thank you for this new day that You have made. Order my steps. Help me, Holy Spirit, to represent my Father well. Bless every participant and attendee. I pray for and thank you for peace, order and favor this day. Thank you for protection to and from and for provision for every need. Demonstrate Your power. Be glorified. Encourage, refresh, restore, comfort, heal. Thank you, Lord. In Jesus' mighty name. Amen. Happy Saturday all!

Posted on Facebook December 14, 2013, 6:38 am

Father God, I thank you that my identity, credit and all personal data is covered and protected as well as of my family. I am not anxious from any news reports for my trust is in You. Thank you, Lord. In Jesus' name. Amen.

Posted on Facebook December 19, 2013, 8:54 am

Father, bless my Morgan State family as they celebrate the life of Jack Dennis. In Jesus' name. Amen.

Posted on Facebook December 24, 2013

Father God, as we celebrate with family and friends the birth of Your Son Jesus, I lift up those who are not merry. Comfort those who have lost a loved one and will experience this holiday season without their presence. Minister peace to those discouraged or depressed. Minister joy to those who feel hopeless. Encourage those who are away from family and friends. Jesus is the reason we can celebrate no matter what situations look like. In Him, we have joy and peace. In Him, we have eternal security. In Him, we can face our tomorrow. Heal the hurting and those hating because of hurt. I pray for those who do not have a personal relationship with You that they would come to receive Your Son as Savior and Lord. Demonstrate Your power this season. Thank you for provision. Thank you for protection. Thank you for loving, forgiving and giving. Bless my family and Facebook friends. In Jesus' name. Amen.

Posted on Facebook December 31, 2013

Father, thank you for this new day that You have made. I celebrate the successes of 2013 and look forward with excitement for what will manifest in 2014. I've grown from mistakes and look forward to continued pruning so I can bear much fruit. Bless my family members, friends, pastors and church family. Demonstrate Your Power in 2014. Use me to be a blessing and be glorified in my life. You are faithful, and I trust You! In Jesus' mighty name, amen! Have a safe NYE all!

2014

Posted on Facebook January 6, 2014

Father God, thank you for this new day that You have made. Order my steps and may my attitude and actions be pleasing to You. Holy Spirit, guide me through this day and use me for Your glory. Thank you for peace, order, productivity and favor this day, week and month. Thank you for unity in our homes, churches, and community. Thank you for protection and provision. Thank you for salvation for our unsaved loved ones. Thank you for rededication, restoration and reconciliation for those discouraged or deceived by the enemy. God, You are faithful. You are more than able to do what You said, what You promised. I trust You and believe You. I stand on Your Word. I expect the supernatural this day, week, month and year. Demonstrate Your Power in our community and our country. Revive us again. Thank you, Lord. In Jesus' mighty name. Amen.

Posted on Facebook January 9, 2014

Father God, thank you for this new day of peace, protection, provision, productivity and power that You have made. Order our steps and orchestrate every activity. Holy Spirit, guide and lead us this day. Bless the preparation, PMT workers, preachers and participants for our revival. I pray for souls to be saved, hearts to be encouraged and lives to be forever changed for Your glory. Thank you, Lord. In Jesus' mighty name. Amen.

Posted on Facebook January 9, 2014

Father God, there is NOTHING impossible for You. I pray Your perfect will for this baby girl and family. I pray for peace and strength through this challenge. Meet every need. Demonstrate Your power, Lord. In Jesus' mighty and matchless name, amen.

Posted on Facebook January 9, 2014

Father God, thank you for a wonderful time of worship and word tonight. I pray for sweet, sound sleep when I finally get to rest. I pray to wake refreshed and renewed in a few hours to carry out every task and assignment in excellence. I pray this for my entire LPCC family. Thank you, Lord. In Jesus' name. Amen.

Posted on Facebook January 10, 2014

Father, comfort those in need right now. In Jesus' name. Amen.

Text to Hubby January 10, 2014, 5:35 am

Father God, thank you for this new day that You have made. You are so faithful God. Give us the Supernatural strength to be effective and efficient in everything we do today. We choose to believe the report of The Lord and Your report says we are healed. I pray for safety throughout this day for every family member, friend and foe. Surround us with peace. Use us to be a blessing to those we come in contact. I thank you for Robert and his love, care, concern and support. Bless our pastors and church family. Thank you for answered prayer. I lift up Radford and Denise to You right now and pray for their salvation and surrender to You. In Jesus' name. Amen.

Text to Hubby January 13, 2014, 5:43 am

Father God, thank you for this new day. Thank you for my husband, my partner in marriage and ministry. Thank you for his love, care, support, concern. Thank you for intimacy and sex with him. Thank you for his encouragement and his selfless giving to his family. Bless Robert from the crown of his head to the soles of his feet. Holy Spirit, lead, guide and direct him. Demonstrate Your power in and through his life. Increase and elevate him. Protect and provide for him. Thank you, Lord, for joining us together. I love You Lord, and I so love him. In Jesus' name. Amen. I love you, Robert!

Posted on Facebook January 14, 2014

Father, You are so faithful. I love You and thank You. Comfort those experiencing the loss of a loved one. Heal those experiencing challenges in their body. Provide for those experiencing lack. Walk with those preparing for a medical procedure. Minister to those experiencing broken relationships. Encourage those experiencing depression and discouragement. Strengthen those experiencing physical, mental or emotional weakness. Thank you, Lord! In Jesus' mighty name, amen.

Posted on Facebook January 15, 2014

Father, thank you for this supernatural shift. Thank you for heart surgery. Thank you for mercy, grace and forgiveness. Guide me this day Holy Spirit. In Jesus' name. Amen!

Posted on Facebook January 16, 2014

Father, convict the driver who caused the accident yesterday at Balboa and Parthenia that resulted in the loss of life so that he would come forward and confess. Comfort the family and friends and meet every need. Thank you, Lord. In Jesus' name. Amen.

Posted on Facebook January 18, 2014

Father God, thank you for this new day that You have made. I pray for peace, protection, provision and productivity throughout this day. I pray for grace for everything that must be done. I pray for wisdom to know what can wait.

Thank you for my family and friends. Bless each one this day. Meet every need. Save. Heal. Comfort. Deliver. Strengthen. Encourage. Rescue. Restore.

Thank you for my Pastors and LPCC family. Minister to and through each of us for Your glory. Demonstrate Your power in every location including Cyber Church. Thank you for the harvest of souls. I give You all the praise, honor and glory. In Jesus' mighty name. Amen. Have a wonderful weekend all!

Posted on Facebook January 20, 2014

Father, thank you for this new day that You have made. Thank you for new mercies. Great is Your faithfulness. Thank you for peace, order and protection this day. Holy Spirit, lead and direct. In Jesus' name. Amen. Have a blessed day! Happy Monday!

Posted on Facebook January 20, 2014

Father, thank you for satisfying me and my family/friends with long life and showing us Your salvation. I pray for Your miraculous hand to move on behalf of the lady leaving the breakfast which had a heart attack. Breathe life into her right now. Minister peace and faith to her family. Prepare the ER to receive her. Thank you, Lord. In Jesus' name. Amen. Pray believers.

Posted on Facebook January 21, 2014

Father, thank you for covering my spirit/emotions. Thank you for Your Joy, Your Strength, Your Peace. Keeping my mind on You. In Jesus' name. Amen.

Posted on Facebook January 21, 2014

Father God, nothing is hidden from You. Reveal all terror threats in Russia before any destruction or death can take place. Cover all Olympic athletes, activities, events, venues and personnel. Thank you, Lord! In Jesus' mighty and matchless name. Amen.

Posted on Facebook January 22, 2014

My faith is fixed, focused and firmly set on my Father, the One and Only, True and Living, Faithful and Forgiving God. I pursue, overtake and recover all this day. No give up, no give in, no give out.

Posted on Facebook January 25, 2014

Father God, comfort the family and friends of the victims in the Columbia Mall shooting as well as the shooter and the victim of the shooting at South Carolina State Univ. Minister healing. In Jesus' name. Amen.

Father God, thank you for this new day that You have made. Thank you for Your hand of protection over us. Thank you for never leaving us or forsaking us. Thank you for forgiving us. Thank you for mercy and grace.

Go before us this day. Order our steps. Orchestrate every activity and arrange every assignment. Surround us with peace throughout this day. Give us wisdom and discernment for every interaction.

We are not moved by what we see but by what we believe. You are still on the throne, and we trust You. You are faithful. You are Lord. You are the Way, the Truth and the Life.

Thank you, Lord! In Jesus' mighty name. Amen. Have a blessed, Holy Spirit led day!

This is the day that The Lord has made. I will rejoice and be glad in it. Father God, I lift up Atlanta and other areas severely impacted by weather conditions to You and pray for safety and wisdom in how to maneuver and adjust. I pray for physical, mental and emotional strength and for every need to be met. Thank you, Lord. In Jesus' name. Amen.

Father God will you open the floodgates of Heaven and let it rain, let it rain. Thank you, Lord.

Father God, California needs a Supernatural downpour to counteract the exceptional drought and mega drought. Shower down on this state and not just in the natural but send a spiritual revival. I pray for hearts receptive to the truth of Your Word, receptive to Your Light and the Hope only You can provide. Have mercy Lord. Thank you for being long-suffering towards us. Show Yourself strong on behalf of Your people. In Jesus', name, amen!

Father God, I lift up Anthem/WellPoint to You and pray for encouragement for all workers. I pray for fair management decisions.

Fill that place with Your refreshing presence. I pray for peace and come against stress, anxiety and low morale. Demonstrate Your power. In Jesus' name. Amen.

Father God, You are THE Great Physician, so I lift up Lais to You and pray for supernatural intervention in her healing. I pray for accurate diagnosis and treatment. I pray for her organs and bodily function to come in line with the Word of God and function properly. Demonstrate Your power and perform the miraculous. Thank you, Lord, for your grace and mercy. In Jesus' mighty name, amen.

Father God, thank you for this new day that You have made. I pray for wonderful, rich and powerful worship and word. I pray for souls to be saved, hearts to be encouraged and lives to be forever changed. Demonstrate Your power this day. I pray for protection and safe travels throughout this day, across the country. I pray for peace and order at the Super Bowl and wherever people gather for fun and enjoyment. I lift up my family and friends today and pray for health, healing and wholeness. I pray for comfort, strength and encouragement. I pray for restoration, reconciliation and redemption. I pray for forgiveness and favor. I pray for provision for every need. I pray for peace and come against demonic interference and distractions. Be glorified in the lives of Your people. Thank you, Lord. In Jesus' mighty name. Amen.

Father God, thank you for this new day that You have made. I pray for order and direction this day. I pray for restoration and reconciliation of God-ordained relationships. I pray for healing from offense and misunderstanding. I pray for wisdom and discernment to govern decisions.

Holy Spirit lead guide and direct us. I thank you in advance for a peaceful and productive day and grace and favor for every assignment. I come against distractions and pray for laser focus. Father, demonstrate

Your power on behalf of Your people. Thank you, Lord. In Jesus' mighty name. Amen.

Posted on Facebook February 6, 2014

Father God, thank you for this new day that You have made. Thank you for grace for every assignment. Thank you for wisdom to know when to say no and supernatural strength when I don't. Thank you for loving, forgiving and favoring me. Thank you for the plans and purpose You have for me. I am open and ready. Be glorified in and through my life. In Jesus' mighty name. Amen.

Posted on Facebook February 9, 2014

Father God, thank you that all things work together for my good because I love You and I am called according to Your purpose.

Posted on Facebook February 11, 2014

Father God, thank you for this new day that you have made. Thank you for favor this day. Thank you for supernatural strength, both physical and mental. Thank you for the fervent, prevailing, powerful prayers of the righteous.

Thank you for double grace for double assignment. Thank you for victory in every area. Thank you that no weapon formed against me, my family or my future shall prosper. Thank you for wisdom and discernment.

Father, I lift up my family, friends and acquaintances to You and pray that You minister to their needs. Bless, comfort, strengthen, encourage, deliver, provide for and heal those in need. I pray a hedge of protection around our schools, around our workplaces and wherever people gather. I come against demonic influence and interactions in the name of Jesus. Demonstrate your power this day in the lives of your people. Thank you, Lord! In Jesus' mighty name, amen. Happy Tuesday and have a blessed day!

Posted on Facebook February 13, 2014

Father God, thank you for this new day that You have made. I pray for and thank you in advance for safe travels to and in Baltimore today because You've given Your angels charge over me. I pray for favor with everyone I come in contact with and speak peace and order over my day. I pray that all is well for my coworkers traveling as well. I come against confusion, frustration, equipment malfunction, accident and all demonic activity/interference. Be glorified this day. Demonstrate Your power this day and weekend. Bless my family and friends. Thank you, Lord. In Jesus' mighty name. Amen.

Posted on Facebook February 13, 2014

Father God, thank you for this adventurous travel day. Thank you for a warm, comfortable, truly blessed home to lay my head down tonight. I pray for sound sleep that I may wake rested and refreshed in the morning to continue my travel to the east coast. In Jesus' name. Amen. Good night all! What a day! Thankful!

Posted on Facebook February 14, 2014

The plane is at the gate. Will be boarding soon. It was a great layover in Phoenix. Father God, thank you for this new day that You have made. Thank you for continued safe travels. Thank you for loving me and showing that love through others. Thank you for blessing my family and keeping them safe. I pray for a smooth flight and safe arrival in Baltimore. I pray for clear, safe roads where I travel. God, you are so faithful. Thank you for favor everywhere I go. I love and trust You. Meet the needs of my family and Facebook friends. Heal, comfort, strengthen, encourage, provide for, deliver. Thank you, Lord. In Jesus' name, I pray. Amen. Happy Friday everyone! Have a wonderful, blessed day and weekend! God loves you and there's nothing you can do about it. That's a good thing!

Posted on Facebook February 16, 2014

Father God, bless every service and demonstrate Your power in miracles, signs and wonders. Pour out Your love in the congregation and heal hearts, minds, bodies and relationships. I may not be present physically as I am traveling back, but I receive everything You have ordained for me. Thank you, Lord. In Jesus' name. Amen.

Posted on Facebook February 17, 2014

Father God, Yes to Your will and Your way. Yes to Your plan and Your purpose. Order my steps. Orchestrate my life. Be glorified in and through my life and demonstrate your power through me. I give only You the praise, honor and glory.

Posted on Facebook February 17, 2014

Father God, thank you for strength, encouragement, courage, determination, wisdom and grace to continue growing and maturing and excelling and producing. I come against discouragement, defeat, confusion, frustration and irritation that leads to stagnation. Thank you, Father for family and community. In Jesus' name. Amen.

Posted on Facebook February 18, 2014

Father God, I lift up Bretta Rucker Morton and Star Morton to You and pray for continued healing. I pray for peace that passes all understanding. I pray for physical, mental and emotional strength to continue to go through and grow through every situation to be all You have called them to be. I come against grief that paralyzes and regret. Minister love and meet each of their needs. Thank you for the life of Cleveland. We are blessed to have known him. Bless his entire family. Thank you, Lord. In Jesus' name. Amen.

Posted on Facebook February 18, 2014

Father God, thank you for the freedoms we enjoy. I pray for the immediate and safe release of Kenneth Bae and others. In Jesus' name, amen.

Posted on Facebook February 19, 2014

Father God, I pray that this movie (God's Not Dead) would minister to both believers and non-believers. I pray for conviction that results in rededication and salvation. I pray for revival and re-commitment to Christ. Cover everyone connected to this movie project. I pray for over-the-top box office sales. Demonstrate Your power, Lord. I come against back lash in the name of Jesus. You are the only true and living God. You are the Way, the Truth and the Life. Thank you for safety and security found only in You. You are faithful and able. I give You all praise, glory and honor. In Jesus' name. Amen.

Posted on Facebook February 19, 2014

Father God, thank you for this new and blessed day that You have made. Help me to walk in wisdom, discretion, discernment, honesty and integrity in all my affairs, interactions and relationships. In Jesus' name. Amen. Happy Wednesday!

Posted on Facebook February 20, 2014

Father God, thank you for this new day that You have made. Thank you for grace and favor this day.

Jehovah Shalom, I thank you peace this day. I thank you for order over every aspect of this day.

Jehovah Jireh, thank you for provision this day. I pray for all in need of a Supernatural breakthrough. Meet the needs of Your people. I pray for those in need of employment and open doors of opportunity.

Jehovah Rapha, thank you for healing, health, and wholeness. I pray for all in need of physical, emotional and mental healing. Demonstrate Your power.

Jehovah Shammah, you never leave or forsake us, and I pray for those in need of comfort, strength and Your tangible presence this day.

I worship and adore You El-Elyon, the Most High God. I bless Your name, El-Shaddai, the God Almighty of Blessings. I bless Your name Adonai, my Lord and Master.

In Jesus' mighty and matchless name. Amen.

Posted on Facebook February 23, 2014

Father God, thank you for this new day that You have made. I will rejoice and be glad in it. Thank you for favor, grace and mercy. Minister to the needs of the people for salvation, healing, comfort, strength, restoration, provision, protection, deliverance, peace. Holy Spirit, have Your way. Bless my family members and friends. Bless my Pastors and church family and friends. Order my steps this day and be glorified in my life. I give you all the glory, honor and praise. In Jesus' mighty name. Amen.

Posted on Facebook February 24, 2014

Father God, thank you for this new day that You have made. I thank you that this day and week is already blessed. I thank you for peace, order, productivity and favor.

I lift up the needs of those calling on You now for salvation, healing, peace, comfort, strength, encouragement, protection, provision, deliverance, breakthrough, intervention, and turnaround. Restore relationships this day.

Thank you, Lord, for hearing and answering. Thank you for never leaving or forsaking us. I give You all the glory, honor and praise. In Jesus' mighty name. Amen.

It's a beautiful morning for my walk. Happy Monday!

Posted on Facebook February 26, 2014

This is the day that the Lord has made. I will rejoice and be glad in it. Father, I thank you for breakthrough, turn around and sudden change in the lives of Your people. I thank you for resources and open doors of opportunity. I thank you that we are not moved by what we see but only by what we believe. Demonstrate Your power on our behalf this day. Thank you, Lord! In Jesus' name, amen.

Posted on Facebook February 28, 2014

Father God, thank you for this new day that You have made. Thank you for health and wholeness. I pray for safe travels from accident and injury on these wet roads and sidewalks. I pray drivers would be cautious and not anxious. Thank you for the rain. Thank you that this day is already blessed and favor-filled. Demonstrate Your power and use me for Your glory. I lift up the needs of my family and FB friends to You. I love, honor and adore You. In Jesus' name. Amen. Happy Friday! Be safe!

Posted on Facebook March 3, 2014

Father, thank you for this new day that You have made. I declare peace, order and favor over my day. My fitness is blessed. My finances are blessed. My family and household are blessed. My future is blessed.

Posted on Facebook March 3, 2014

Father God, I thank you that LPCC Santa Clarita is flourishing and overflowing with all who You've called to serve Your Kingdom in this location. I thank you that the auditorium is filled to capacity every week. I thank you for hungry souls with hearts ready to receive. I thank you for workers in abundance to minister to the harvest. I thank you that Pastor Sylvester and Lady Antoinette Bell are anointed and appointed to carry out this assignment. I praise You, Father, because You are faithful and the complete vision You have for LPCC shall be fulfilled. Bless our Pastors, Dr. Fred and Linda Hodge, and the entire church family. In Jesus' name. Amen.

Posted on Facebook March 4, 2014

I'm on assignment. Father God, thank you for this day that You have made. I declare peace, order and favor over this day and I come against demonic influence and activity. Thank you for victory, turnaround and sudden change. In the mighty and matchless name of Jesus, I pray. Amen and Amen.

Posted on Facebook March 7, 2014

Father God, thank you for this new day that You have made. This day is blessed, peaceful, orderly and productive. My family is blessed. My fitness is blessed. My finances are blessed. My future is blessed. I am diligent and walk in discipline and self-control in every area. Father, thank you for favor. Thank you for protection, provision and promotion. Thank you for the shift. Use me for Your glory and demonstrate Your power in and through my life. You are so faithful. I praise, honor, glorify and magnify You. In Jesus' mighty and matchless name. Amen.

Posted on Facebook March 9, 2014

Father God, thank you for this new day that You have made. Thank you for the lives that will be changed for the better this day. Minister through every gift and expression of worship. Save souls, heal hearts, restore relationships. Thank you, Lord. In Jesus' name. Amen.

Posted on Facebook March 9, 2014

I'm a cyber evangelist sent to terrorize the forces of the kingdom of darkness.

Posted on Facebook March 13, 2014

Father God, thank you for this blessed day that You have made. I am glad and grateful for it. I declare peace, order, productivity, and favor over my day and come against distractions, confusion, and delay. I love, honor, praise and adore You, Lord. In Jesus' mighty name, amen. Have an amazing day!

Posted on Facebook March 14, 2014

Father God, thank you for this new day that You have made. I pray for safe travels going to and coming from Riley's Farm with the 5th graders and a good day. Thank you, Lord. In Jesus' name. Amen.

Posted on Facebook March 17, 2014

Father God, we are anxious for nothing and our confidence and trust is in You. We seek You for direction and wisdom. We thank you for protection. We thank you for warning signs. Demonstrate Your power in our lives. Be glorified this day. In Jesus' name. Amen. God is faithful, y'all!

Posted on Facebook March 19, 2014

Father God, thank you for this new day that You have made. Thank you for another year of life. Thank you for forty-five blessed years. Thank you for never leaving or forsaking me. Thank you for favor over my life. Thank you for ordering my steps and directing the path I should take. Thank you for peace, protection, provision and promotion. Thank you for Your plans to prosper me. Use me for Your glory and continue to demonstrate Your power in and through my life. I love You, Lord. I give You all praise, honor and glory. In Jesus' name. Amen. Grateful!

Father God, thank you for this blessed day that You have made. Thank you for the harvest of souls and laborers to serve in every location. I call in workers to meet every need. I thank you for an abundance of resources in every PMT department. I thank you for double grace for double ministry. I thank you for balance. I thank you for supernatural strength for every assignment. Thank you, Lord, for miracles, signs and wonders. You are faithful. In Jesus' mighty name. Amen. Hallelujah!

Father God, thank you for this new day that You have made. Thank you for this week of impact, power and turnaround. We are not moved by what we see but by what believe. We stand on Your Word. We trust in You. Thank you for peace, protection, provision and promotion this week. Demonstrate Your power on behalf of Your people. Use us for Your glory. In Jesus' mighty and matchless name. Amen.

Father God, thank you for this blessed day that You have made. Thank you for victory, turnaround and sudden change. Thank you for miracles, signs, and wonders.

I lift up to You all in need right now. I pray for those in need of employment. I pray for open doors of opportunity. I pray for favor with every decision maker. Jehovah Jireh, be their Provider.

I pray for those in need of salvation. I pray they would come to a saving grace knowledge of You and secure an eternal home in heaven. You are the way, the truth, and life. You are the hope they need.

I pray for those in need of a miraculous move of God in their bodies. I pray every organ line up according to the Word of God and every named diagnosis bow to the name of Jesus. I pray for accurate diagnosis where needed. Demonstrate Your healing power Jehovah Rapha.

I lift up marriages to You and pray that husbands and wives would seek You for direction and submit to your guidance. I pray for healing and restoration where there is separation or divorce. Heal the pain from hurtful words or actions.

Father God, comfort, encourage, strengthen those in need. I come against depression, despair, discouragement, and thoughts of suicide. Saturate them with Your peace and love. Invade their darkness with Your light.

I lift up those in need of a church home where they can grow and fellowship with other believers and sow and serve in Your Kingdom. Heal hurt and restore relationships. May they return to their set place.

Thank you, Father! You are faithful. In Jesus' mighty name I pray. Amen.

Posted on Facebook March 26, 2014

Father God, thank you for this new day. Thank you for peace, order, productivity and favor. Thank you for protection and provision. Thank you for health and wholeness.

Posted on Facebook March 28, 2014

Father God, thank you for this new day that You have made. Thank you for mercy and grace. Thank you for peace, order and favor this day. I am excited and in expectation over what You've done and what You're about to do in the lives of Your people. I give You all glory, honor and praise. In Jesus' mighty and matchless name. Amen.

Posted on Facebook March 29, 2014

Father God, thank you for this new day. Have Your way this day. Be glorified in my life and use me for Your glory. Demonstrate Your power this day and this weekend. You are so faithful. I love you and trust You. Bless my family, friends, pastors and church family. Thank you, Lord. In Jesus' mighty name, amen. Happy Saturday! Have a wonderful weekend!

Posted on Facebook April 3, 2014

Father God, thank you for this new day that You have made. I thank you that this day is already blessed. I thank you for peace, order, productivity, and favor over this day. I thank you for healing in my body. I thank you for protection. I thank you for turn-around and victory in every area. Thank you for loving me, forgiving me and never leaving or forsaking me. You are faithful, and I trust You. Bless and meet the needs of those calling on You right now. Heal, save, deliver, comfort, encourage, strengthen, provide for the needs of Your people. Bless my family and friends. Bless my Pastors and church family. Thank you, Lord, for Supernatural miracles, signs, and wonders this day. In Jesus' mighty name. Amen.

Posted on Facebook April 4, 2014

Father God, I thank you for the blessing of family and friendship. I thank you for mutually beneficial, God-ordained relationships. I thank you for fulfillment of purpose and destiny. I come against delays and distractions and commit to being diligent and determined to carry out Your assignment for my life. Demonstrate Your power and use me for Your glory. No weapon formed against me, my family, my fitness, my finances or my future shall prosper. Thank you, Lord. Thank you for victory, turnaround and sudden change this day/season. In Jesus' mighty name. Amen.

Posted on Facebook April 6, 2014

Father God, thank you for this new and blessed day that You have made. Thank you for continued and complete healing in my body. In Jesus' mighty name. Amen.

Posted on Facebook April 7, 2014

Father God, thank you for this new day that You have made filled with fresh grace and mercy. Great is Your faithfulness indeed. I thank you that no weapon formed against me, my family, my fitness or my future will prosper. I declare peace, order, productivity and favor over this day. My day is blessed, and I walk in divine health and prosper as my soul prospers. I thank you that every organ function in perfection as You created them to function and by Jesus' stripes I AM HEALED. Thank you for going before me to make the crooked places straight. Thank you for hearing and answering this day. Be glorified in my life and use me for Your glory. In Jesus' mighty name. Amen. Happy Blessed Monday!

Posted on Facebook April 8, 2014

Father, You are faithful, and I trust you. Help me to be diligent and walk in wisdom and discernment. Thank you, Lord. In Jesus' name. Amen.

Posted on Facebook April 9, 2014

Father God, thank you for this new day that You have. I rejoice and am glad in it. I thank you for the shift and trust You to work all things out for my good and Your glory. I pray for wisdom and diligence through the process. I thank you for mercy and grace. Help me to be who You've called me to be and do what You've called me to do. I am listening.

Father, heal those in need of Your supernatural touch. I pray for miracles, signs and wonders to manifest in their body, mind and emotions. Comfort those in need of peace, strength and encouragement to make it through the loss of life or relationship. Provide finances, resources and favor for those who are stretched and in need of food, clothes and shelter. Open doors of employment and opportunity for those without a job or the best job. Restore relationships impacted by lies and deception. Deliver from darkness, depression and discouragement. Minister to the needs of Your people. Father, I thank you for going before me to make the crooked places straight. I thank you for continued healing, protection, and provision. I thank you for peace, order, productivity and favor over my day and week. Be glorified. I thank You and trust You. In Jesus' mighty and matchless name I pray. Amen!

Posted on Facebook April 10, 2014

Father God, thank you for this new day that You have made. I thank you for continued healing and supernatural strength. I declare this day blessed. In Jesus' name. Amen.

Posted on Facebook April 11, 2014

Father God, thank you for this new day that You have made. I pray for safe, timely travel for the volunteers, teams, and presidents making their way to California for HCASC this weekend. Thank you, Lord. In Jesus' name. Amen.

Posted on Facebook April 12, 2014

Father God, I truly need a Supernatural touch/healing and restoration of my voice. I pray for sound sleep and rest. I pray for mental and physical strength for every HCASC participant this weekend. Thank you, Lord. In Jesus' name. Amen.

Posted on Facebook April 13, 2014

Father, thank you for seeing me through this day. My voice is stronger than last night this time. Thank you for healing and wholeness. Bless my family, friends, pastors and church family. In Jesus' name with thanksgiving. Amen.

Posted on Facebook April 17, 2014

Father God, thank you for this new day that You have made. You are so faithful and forgiving. I stand in awe of You! You are awesome and amazing. You are almighty and all powerful. You are compassionate and caring. I love You, trust You and will serve You all the days of my life. Order my steps. Bless my family and friends. In Jesus' mighty name. Amen.

Posted on Facebook April 19, 2014

Father God, thank you for this day that You have made. Thank you for new grace and fresh mercy. Thank you for forgiveness of sin.

I call this day blessed. I pray for peace, protection and productivity throughout this day. Use me for Your glory, order my steps and direct my path. Thank you for wisdom and discernment.

I pray for souls to be saved, hearts to be healed and lives to be forever changed for the better this weekend. Bless, comfort, encourage, deliver, save, heal and provide for those calling on You now. Demonstrate Your power this day. Thank you, Lord. In Jesus' mighty name. Amen.

Happy Resurrection Weekend all! He died for you/us so that you/we can live eternally with Him. God's not dead. Jesus lives forever. Holy Spirit leads and guides the believer. If you haven't, accept/receive His free gift of salvation while you can. Have a wonderful weekend!

Posted on Facebook April 21, 2014

Father God, thank you for this new day that You have made and another work week. I declare peace, order, productivity and favor over this week. This day and week is blessed. I pray for safety over our schools as they return from spring break. I pray both staff and students are prepared to be successful. I come against demonic activity and interference. I pray a hedge of protection in the classrooms, on the playground, and in the neighborhoods. I plead the blood of Jesus over our schools and our workplaces. Thank you, Lord. You, Father, are faithful. I love and trust You. In Jesus' name. Amen.

Posted on Facebook April 23, 2014

Father God, thank you for this new day that You have made. Thank you for supernatural healing. Thank you for turnaround, sudden change and victory in every area. I am not moved by what I see but only by what I believe. I believe that You are causing all things to work together for my good and Your glory. Demonstrate Your power in my life and the lives of my family members and friends. Thank you, Lord, for this day blessed with peace, productivity, and favor. In Jesus' mighty name. Amen. Happy Wednesday!

Posted on Facebook April 23, 2014

Father God, thank you for this new day, new season of victory, turnaround and sudden change. In expectation of great things. You are faithful, and I trust You. Thank you for sweet sleep and wonderful rest. In Jesus' name. Amen.

Posted on Facebook April 24, 2014

Father God, thank you for this new day of VICTORY. Thank you for breakthrough, turnaround and sudden change. Thank you for the shift. Thank you for the powerful ministry and praise reports on the LPCC prayer line. I am in expectation. Thank you for peace, productivity, protection and provision this day. Use me for your glory. In the mighty and matchless name of Jesus, I pray with thanksgiving. Amen.

Posted on Facebook April 24, 2014

Father God, I thank you for You are faithful and promise never to leave us or forsake us. I lift up all in need of Your touch right now.

I pray for those needing physical, mental, emotional or relational healing. I know You to be a healer. I pray for accurate diagnosis and treatment. I pray for successful surgeries. I come against complications, infections and premature death.

I lift up those who've lost a loved one and those in the midst of a family member's transition. Surround them with peace and comfort. Strengthen and encourage.

I lift up those in need of basic needs. Provide food, clothes and shelter. Provide open doors of opportunity and employment. Show them favor with creditors. Blow their minds.

I come against fear, torment, depression and discouragement. I pray for joy and peace only You can provide. Demonstrate Your power this day. Thank you, Lord. In Jesus' mighty name. Amen.

Posted on Facebook April 27, 2014

Father God, thank you for this new day that You have made. Thank you for brand new mercies this day. There is no one like You, no one greater than You. Thank you for this new season. You are so faithful. Thank you for never leaving or forsaking me/us. Help me to be who You've called me to be and do what You've called me to do.

Father, I lift up my family and friends and my Pastors and church family and their family members to You and pray that You move in their lives. You know the need. Bless, heal, save, comfort, deliver, encourage, strengthen, provide for, restore, mend, rebuild, favor, bring clarity, rescue.

Go before us this day to make the crooked places straight. Order our steps and use us for your glory. I pray that souls are saved, hearts are healed and encouraged, and lives are forever changed. Be glorified in the lives of Your servants and ministry gifts. Bless every worker serving in Your kingdom. Holy Spirit, have Your way. Demonstrate Your power with miracles, signs, and wonders.

Thank you, Lord! In Jesus' mighty name. Amen.

Posted on Facebook April 28, 2014

Father God, thank you for this new day that You have made. Thank you for brand new mercies. Great is Your faithfulness. I thank you this day is blessed, and I speak peace, order and productivity over my day. I thank you for favor and fulfillment of purpose.

Minister to and provide for those in need of salvation, healing, comfort, shelter, deliverance, restoration, employment, strength. Thank you, Lord. In Jesus' mighty name. Amen.

Posted on Facebook April 29, 2014

Father God, I thank you that you are the Great Physician and Healer. I lift up my mom to You and all those preparing for any medical procedure. I pray or accurate diagnosis and treatment. I pray for the best medical team for whatever needs to take place. I pray against complications and delays. I pray for complete and quick healing and recovery without infection or setback. I also lift up those experiencing health challenges that have not yet been properly diagnosed that You would give direction and wisdom for proper treatment. I pray for miracles, signs, and wonders. Be glorified and demonstrate Your power. Father, I pray for peace to rule their hearts and minds. I come against fear and pray that they stand in faith believing You are faithful. Thank you, Lord. In Jesus' mighty name, amen.

Posted on Facebook May 1, 2014

Father God, thank you for this new day that You have made. Thank you for another month and season. I pray that America would return to righteousness. I pray that we, Your people, would humble ourselves, seek Your face, turn from our wicked ways as we pray. You promise to hear from heaven, forgive our sin and heal our land. Our land needs healing.

I plead the blood of Jesus over our schools, our churches, our homes, our communities, our workplaces and everywhere we transact business. I pray for protection from demonic influenced activity. I pray for a return to godly principles.

Father, You wish that none perish. I pray for repentance and salvation of our loved ones. I pray for submission to Your Holy Spirit. I thank you that as we submit, You shall make our plans prosperous and successful. I pray for victory, turnaround and sudden change this day. Demonstrate Your power this day. Be glorified in our lives this day. In Jesus' mighty name. Amen.

Posted on Facebook May 3, 2014

Father God, I lift up the LAPD and pray for comfort of all officers and the family members of all those who've lost their lives this year alone. Comfort each one. I pray for protection and safety. I pray this for all law enforcement across the country. In Jesus' name. Amen.

Posted on Facebook May 4, 2014

Father God, thank you for this new day that You have made. Thank you for brand new mercy and grace. Thank you for protection from dangers seen and unseen. Thank you for never leaving us or forsaking us. Thank you for watching over us. Thank you for the broken body and shed blood of Your Son Jesus for our healing and salvation.

Father God, I lift up my family and friends to You and plead the blood of Jesus and pray a hedge of protection over each one. I pray for salvation, repentance, reconciliation, deliverance from depression, guilt and self-sabotage. I pray for comfort, strength, encouragement and physical, mental, spiritual and emotional healing.

Father, I pray for quick and complete healing without complications or setbacks for those who have had surgery. I pray for miracles, signs and wonders for those who've received a dire report. I pray for accuracy in diagnosis and treatment for those who need to know what an on going challenging issue is. Jehovah, demonstrate Your power. Heal bodies, minds and emotions this day.

Father, I lift up those needing food, clothing and shelter. Provide for those needing employment, promotion or increase. Father, open doors of opportunity. Restore hope. Provide benefits.

Thank you, Lord, for hearing and answering. Thank you for victory, turnaround and sudden change. Thank you for peace in this already blessed day. Be glorified this day. Thank you, Lord. In Jesus' mighty name. Amen.

Posted on Facebook May 4, 2014

Father God, thank you for new insight on worship. I praise You for your vessel, Minister Tamara Joy Scott. You are so on time. You are so faithful. I love You, honor You and adore You. In Jesus' mighty name. Amen. Hallelujah!

Posted on Facebook May 4, 2014

Father God, thank you for this wonderful day. It was filling and enriching from start to finish. You are awesome and amazing. I thank you for victory, turnaround and sudden change in my life and family. I submit and surrender to Your plan, purpose and process for my life. You are faithful, and I trust You. Give us sound sleep and sweet rest after this powerful day of ministry. Bless, heal, save, comfort, deliver and provide for my family and friends. In Jesus' mighty name. Amen. Good night all. Sleep well.

Posted on Facebook May 8, 2014

Father God, I lift up our WOVEN Advance to You and pray for every participant. I pray for safe travels going, returning and throughout the weekend. I pray for wonderful ministry, fellowship and relaxation. Exceed our expectations. Minister to and meet every need. Provide for every financial and family need. Demonstrate Your power and heal hearts, minds and bodies. Thank you for our WOVEN President, Pastor Linda Hodge. Bless her to be a blessing. Move through her mightily. Thank you, Lord. We give You all honor, glory and praise. In Jesus' name. Amen.

Posted on Facebook May 9, 2014

Father God, thank you for this new and wonderfully blessed day that You have made. Order our steps this day. Provide supernatural strength for the 6:30 am boot camp and everything else that will take place today. Bless every speaker and ministry gift. Touch every lady and meet every need. Bless our families and our homes. Have Your way this day. In Jesus' mighty name. Amen. Happy Friday!

Posted on Facebook May 10, 2014

Father God, thank you for this blessed day that You have made. Thank you for never leaving or forsaking us. Thank you for family and friends who support and encourage us. Thank you for parents, pastors, and mentors who guide, challenge and inspire us. Thank you for purpose and potential You placed in us. Thank you for plans to prosper us and bring us to an expected end. Thank you for being faithful and forgiving. I submit to the plan, purpose and process that You have designed for me. Help me to be, do, experience and accomplish all that You have predestined for me. Use me to be a blessing. Demonstrate Your power through me. Be glorified in my life. Bless, save, heal, comfort, encourage, deliver, strengthen, provide for my family and friends in need this day. In Jesus' mighty name. Amen.

Posted on Facebook May 10, 2014

Father God, thank you for the 3-day womens' retreat at the WOVEN Advance. I lift up every lady who attended. I pray that the healing that took place will continue. I pray for wholeness in the hearts and minds of Your women. Bless and rest Pastor Linda. Increase and overflow in her life. Minister to those ladies who wanted to attend or planned to attend but did not make it. Strengthen WOVEN so that we can be who You have called us to be both individually and as a unit. Use us for Your glory. Thank you, Lord. In Jesus' name. Amen. #wovenadvance2014

Proverbs 14:34 Amplified Bible (AMP)

Uprightness and right standing with God (moral and spiritual rectitude in every area and relation) elevate a nation, but sin is a reproach to any people.

Father God, thank you for this new day that You have made. Create in me a clean heart. Renew a right spirit within me. Forgive me of my sin in word, thought or deed. Help me to be pleasing to You. Thank you for mercy and grace. In Jesus' name. Amen.

Tuesday morning walk even earlier than yesterday. Father God, thank you for this new day that You have made. Thank you for being my Provider, my Protector and my Peace. Thank you for being my Shepherd, my Salvation and my Security. Thank you for being my Healer and my Help in time of need. Thank you for being my Shield and my Strong Tower. Thank you for being my Comforter, my Deliverer and my Way-maker. You are Awesome and

Amazing. You are Faithful and Forgiving. I give You all glory, honor and praise. You are all powerful, all knowing and ever present. There is no one greater than You. Thank you! In Your Son Jesus' mighty name, I pray. Amen

Father God, I lift up my niece and every college student working to finish their semester strong. I pray for supernatural physical and mental strength especially for those holding down jobs and families. I pray for a healthy balance to eat properly, rest, study, rest, work, rest. Give hem clarity of thought to complete all papers, projects, and assignments without struggle or strain. Give them excellent recall of what was taught and studied during the semester to be able to pass every exam. Keep them in perfect peace as they keep their mind stayed on You.

Protect and keep safe everyone celebrating at proms and graduations. May they make wise decisions. I come against premature death and loss of life. Continue to cover our children from daycare through high school. Thank you, Lord. In Jesus' name. Amen.

Posted on Facebook May 14, 2014

My family is blessed. My finances are blessed. My fitness is blessed. My future is bright and blessed. I always win. I can't lose because there is no failure in my Father. I submit to His plan, purpose and process to bring me to His expected end. Excited and in expectation... what's your declaration? I am not moved by what I see or hear but only by what I believe. I believe God!

Posted on Facebook May 18, 2014

Father God, thank you for this blessed day that You have made. Demonstrate Your power this day. Save souls, heal bodies, hearts and minds. Change lives and restore relationships. Thank you, Lord! We love, honor and adore you. In Jesus' name. Amen.

Posted on Facebook May 23, 2014

Dear Heavenly Father, thank you for this new day that You have made. Thank you for new grace and mercy. Thank you for bringing us to the end of another work week.

I declare peace, order, productivity and favor over this day and weekend for my family and friends. I pray for protection during this season of celebrations and the holiday weekend and come against accident, injury and premature death.

Father, meet the needs for salvation, comfort, healing, provision, strength, direction, deliverance, peace, joy, reconciliation, restoration, employment, increase, promotion, miracles. You are faithful. You are forgiving.

Thank you for Your plans for my life. Thank you that Your purpose for my life will manifest. Bless my Pastors and church family, my coworkers and colleagues, my family, friends, and acquaintances.

This is the day that You have made. I rejoice and am glad in it. I praise You, love You and Thank you, Lord. In Jesus' mighty name. Amen. Happy Blessed Friday!

Posted on Facebook May 24, 2014

Father God, thank you for this wonderful day. It was long but productive. Give us sweet sleep and peaceful rest.

I lift up to You the family and friends of those who lost their lives at UCSB as well as the family members of the shooter. Comfort, strengthen and encourage each one. Heal hearts and minds.

You are faithful and can be trusted. I pray for miracles, signs, and wonders to manifest in the lives of Your people. Save souls, heal hearts, change lives and restore relationships. Thank you, Lord. In Jesus' name. Amen.

Posted on Facebook May 25, 2014

Father, thank you for this new day that You have made. Thank you for brand new mercies. Order my steps this day. Use me for Your glory. Holy Spirit, have Your way. Thank you, Lord. In Jesus' name. Amen. Have an amazing day!

Posted on Facebook May 27, 2014

Father God, thank you for this new day that is already blessed. Thank you for peace, order, productivity and favor over this day and work week.

Minister strength, comfort and healing to the family members and friends of every military personnel who gave their life or limb for this country. Touch every troop who continue to suffer from the impact of war. You are The Healer. Demonstrate Your power in bodies, minds, and relationships.

I lift up family members and friends in need of salvation, healing, comfort, deliverance, provision. You are faithful and can be trusted. Thank you for satisfying us with long life and showing us Your salvation.

Thank you for never leaving or forsaking us. Thank you for protection going out and coming in. Thank you for restoring broken, damaged, fractured relationships.

Be glorified in and through my life. I submit to Your plan, purpose and process. Thank you for mercy, grace and forgiveness. Help me to be diligent, disciplined and determined in every area. I give You all praise, honor and glory. Thank you, Lord. In Jesus' name. Amen. Happy Monday!

Posted on Facebook May 28, 2014

Father God, thank you for this new day that You have made. Thank you for purpose and destiny. Thank you for manifestation of God-ordained dreams and desires. Thank you for open doors of opportunity. Thank you that our vision shall come to pass. Help us to remain focused and steadfast on the assignment that You have called us to do. Help us to not get weary in well doing. Help us to be faithful stewards over everything and everyone You've entrusted to us. Thank you for physical, mental, and emotional strength and stamina to accomplish everything. Thank you for putting Your Super on our natural. Thank you for books and businesses, ministries and movies. You are faithful and can be trusted. I love, honor and adore You. In Jesus' mighty and matchless name. Amen.

Posted on Facebook May 30, 2014

Father God, thank you for this new day that You have made. Thank you for protection for family and friends in the air, on the sea or land. Thank you for peace, order and favor. Thank you for provision and productivity. Order my steps and orchestrate every activity. You are faithful, and I trust You. Bless, save, heal, comfort, strengthen and encourage those in need. Thank you, Lord. In Jesus' name. Amen. Have a great, God-ordained day of destiny!

Posted on Facebook July 1, 2014

Father God, thank you for protection. I pray for accuracy in diagnosis and treatment and complete healing. I pray for the restoration of everything that was lost and favor through the process. You are faithful. Thank you, Lord. In Jesus' name. Amen

Posted on Facebook July 11, 2014

Father God, thank you for this blessed day of victory that You have made. I am grateful and glad in it. I am in expectation of rich impartation, wisdom, insight, and revelation. Be glorified Father. In Jesus' mighty name. Amen. Happy Blessed Friday!

Posted on Facebook July 14, 2014

This is the day that The Lord has made. I will rejoice and be glad in it. Father, thank you for this blessed day and week of victory, peace, and productivity. There is greatness in me because I have Your DNA. I come against distractions, demonic activities, and delays to destiny. I thank you for protection, provision, and promotion. Bless my family and friends and demonstrate Your power in the lives of your people. Thank you for breakthrough, turnaround and sudden change. Use me for Your glory. In Jesus' mighty name. Amen! Happy Monday!

Posted on Facebook July 16, 2014

Father God, I thank you for this blessed day of victory that You have made. I rejoice and am grateful and glad in it. I thank you for health, healing, and wholeness in every area. I thank you that every organ functions as You created each to function. I thank you for Your plans to prosper me. I thank you that no weapon formed against me shall prosper. I thank you that I am blessed going out and coming in. I thank you that I am the head and not the tail, above only and not beneath. I thank you that all things are possible with you. I thank you that I can do all things through Christ who strengthens me. I thank you that You have not given me the spirit of fear but of power, love and a sound, well-balanced mind. I thank you that all my needs are met according to Your riches in glory. I thank you that my set time for favor is now. I thank you for promotion, increase, abundance and overflow. Demonstrate Your power in and through my life and use me for Your glory. I lift up my family, friends, pastors and church family and pray the same for them. Have Your way this day. In Jesus' mighty name, amen!

Posted on Facebook July 17, 2014

Father God, thank you for this blessed day that You have made. I lift up those in need of a touch from You right now. I pray for salvation, healing provision, peace, protection, deliverance, restoration, employment, and promotion. I pray for mental and physical strength. I pray for joy to be restored. Rescue the lost, hopeless, deceived and confused. You are faithful and can be trusted. Thank you, Lord. In Jesus' name. Amen.

Posted on Facebook July 20, 2014

Father God, thank you for a wonderful family weekend topped off with an amazing worship experience at the Sound of Victory concert. I'm looking forward to a blessed, productive week. Thank you, Lord! In Jesus' name, amen.

Posted on Facebook July 21, 2014

I'm walking in victory. Father God, You, are Jehovah Rapha, and by Jesus' stripes I am healed and whole. I thank you that every joint, muscle, tendon, cartilage, ligament, cell, tissue, nerve, artery, organ in my body function pain, inflammation, spasm, growth, dysfunction, loss of function or mis-diagnosis in Jesus' name. I prosper and am in health as my soul prospers. I will fulfill the plans and purpose and complete the process You have ordained for me. I can through Christ. Thank you, Lord. In Jesus' mighty and matchless name. Amen.

Posted on Facebook July 23, 2014

Father God, thank you for this new, blessed day of victory and destiny. All things work together for my good and Your glory. Thank you for divine assignments, connections, and intersections. Thank you for satisfying me with long, healthy, abundant life and showing me Your salvation. Thank you, Lord, for brand new mercies. Thank you for never leaving or forsaking me. Thank you for Your love, care, forgiveness and favor. God, You are so faithful.

I lift up my family members, friends, pastors, church family, colleagues and associates to You and pray for a mighty move of God in their lives. I pray for healing and restoration. I pray for salvation and deliverance. I pray for provision, protection, promotion and peace. I pray for comfort, strength, and encouragement. God, You can be trusted.

This is the day that The Lord has made. We rejoice, and we are glad in it. We thank You. We bless Your name. We honor You. We love You. We adore You. We submit to You. We glorify You and magnify You above every situation and circumstance.

Thank you, Lord. In Jesus' mighty and matchless name. Amen.

Posted on Facebook July 23, 2014

Father God, nothing is hidden from You. You see all and know. Reveal the meaning and the responsible party. Protect America and its borders. I pray for Godly guidance for our government. Thank you, Lord. In Jesus' name. Amen.

Posted on Facebook July 24, 2014

Father God, thank you for this blessed day of victory, breakthrough, turnaround and sudden change. You are faithful and able to do exceeding, abundantly above all we think or ask. Thank you for complete healing and total restoration. Thank you for forgiving and favoring me. Thank you for fresh grace and mercies. Be glorified in the lives of Your people this day.

I pray for salvation, healing, comfort, deliverance, provision, protection, promotion, peace and increase for those in need. I pray for broken relationships to be restored and come against offense and deception causing delays to destiny. Thank you, Lord, for hearing and answering. We love You and honor You and bless Your name. In Jesus' name. Amen.

Posted on Facebook July 28, 2014

Walking in victory! Father God, thank you for this blessed day of victory and favor that You have made. You are faithful, and I bless and honor Your name. There is no one greater than You. Your promises are yes and amen. You watch over Your Word to perform it, so I stand on Your word. Thank you for forgiveness, mercy, and grace. I am blessed going out and coming in. I am the head and not the tail. I am the lender and not the borrower. I am the righteousness of God in Christ Jesus. I can do all things through Christ who strengthens me. I walk in divine health and prosper as my soul prospers. By Jesus' stripes, I am healed. No weapon formed against my family or me shall prosper. You have given Your angels charge over me. You satisfy me with long life and show me Your salvation. I shall not die prematurely but live to declare the mighty works of The Lord. I decree and declare peace, order, favor and productivity over my day and week. I thank you for protection, promotion, and provision for every need and even desire as I delight in You. Use me for Your glory and demonstrate Your power in and through my life. You are faithful, and I trust You. Bless my family, friends, pastors and church family. Thank you for miracles, signs, and wonders. In Jesus' mighty and matchless name. Amen. Happy Blessed Monday FB!

Posted on Facebook July 29, 2014

Walking by faith and not by sight. Father, thank you for this blessed day of victory, increase, and expansion that You have made. We bless, honor and exalt Your name. Thank you for enlarging our territory. Thank you for kingdom promotion. We are excited about new opportunities to be used for Your glory. Thank you for open doors without opposition and with all sufficiency. Thank you for every need being met. Thank you for grace for every assignment and diligence to carry it out in excellence.

Father, save, heal, deliver, comfort, protect, encourage and provide for those calling on You now. I lift up the lost and hurting to You. Give them peace and restore their joy. You are faithful, and I trust You.

I pray for wisdom, understanding, and discernment and come against confusion, irritation, and frustration that would delay destiny being fulfilled. Be glorified this day. Thank you, Lord, for hearing and answering. In Jesus' mighty name. Amen.

Posted on Facebook July 29, 2014

Father God, You know everything, and You know her situation, condition, and location. Restore, heal, protect and reconnect her with her loved ones. Thank you, Lord. In Jesus' name, amen.

Posted on Facebook July 30, 2014

Father God, thank you for this day. Thank you for never leaving or forsaking me. Thank you for health, healing, and wholeness. Thank you for protection and provision. I pray You orchestrate my complete recovery and facilitate further treatment with a timely appointment and accurate diagnosis and treatment. By Jesus' stripes, I am healed. Nothing has caught You by surprise. I trust You. Thank you, Lord! In Jesus' name. Amen.

Posted on Facebook August 1, 2014

Father God, I thank you that NO WEAPON formed against me shall prosper. I thank you for satisfying me with long, healthy, abundant life and showing me Your salvation. I thank you that I walk in health and prosper as my soul prospers. I thank you that I shall not die but live to declare the mighty works of the Lord and declare them I shall. I am not moved by what I see or hear but only by what I believe. I am a child of the King, and the enemy is defeated. I am more than a conqueror and can do all things through Christ who strengthens me. I plead the blood of Jesus over my body from the crown of my head to the soles of my feet. Every organ functions in perfection as You Lord created them to function. July is behind me, and my amazing future is before me. Greater is HE who is in me than he who is in the world. My fitness is blessed. My family is blessed. My finances are blessed. My future is blessed. I am victorious. Demonstrate Your Power, Lord. Use me for Your glory. Thank you, Lord! In Jesus' mighty and matchless name, amen.

Posted on Facebook August 4, 2014

Father God, thank you for this new day of victory and blessings that You have made. I rejoice. I am grateful. I am glad. I thank you that no weapon formed against me or my family or my future shall prosper.

You promise in your Word to satisfy me with long life and show me your salvation. Every organ in my body functions in perfection as you created to function and I walk in divine health and prosper. I thank you for accurate diagnosis and treatment and supernatural miracles, signs, and wonders. Demonstrate Your power in and through my life. Meet the needs of every believer calling on You now. You are faithful! Thank you, Lord. In Jesus' mighty, amen. Have a blessed, favor-filled week and month!

Posted on Facebook August 5, 2014

Father God, thank you for this new day that You have made. I plead the blood of Jesus over this day and pray that You go before us to guide and to guard. Order our steps and orchestrate our day. Thank you for brand new mercies.

Father, I lift up those in need of hope right now and pray that You invade their atmosphere and saturate them with Your peace that passes all understanding. I come against the spirit of suicide and pray they be satisfied with long life. There is power in the name of Jesus. I pray for that one in need of salvation. I pray they call on Your Son and receive Him as Savior and Lord. I come against despair, depression, and discouragement and pray for Your joy to strengthen and encourage hearts and minds.

Father, I lift up those whose body is wrecking with pain and pray that You heal from the crown of their head to the soles of their feet. I pray for accurate diagnosis and treatment. I pray for safe, successful surgery. I pray for Your supernatural power to turn situations. I pray for miracles, signs, and wonders to be manifested.

You are faithful. Thank you, Lord, for hearing and answering. In Jesus' mighty name. Amen. God is faithful and can be trusted. Happy Tuesday!

Posted on Facebook August 5, 2014

Father God, thank you for the plans You have for me. Use me for Your glory. Thank you that NO WEAPON formed against me, my family, finances or fitness shall prosper. Thank you for satisfying my family and me with long, healthy, abundant life and showing us Your salvation. In Jesus' name. Amen.

Posted on Facebook August 8, 2014

Father God, thank you for this new, blessed day that You have made. Thank you for this new season. Thank you for favor, peace, and victory. Thank you for promotion, increase, and elevation. Thank you for wisdom, understanding, and discernment. Thank you for manifestation. Thank you for Your plans to prosper me. Use me for Your glory and demonstrate Your power in and through me. In Jesus' mighty name. Amen.

Posted on Facebook August 8, 2014

Father, give us sweet, sound sleep so we can wake rested and refreshed to have a productive day blessed with peace, favor, increase and overflow. Thank you, Lord! In Jesus' name. Amen. Good night and God Bless!

Posted on Facebook August 11, 2014

Father God, thank you for this blessed day of victory that You have made. Thank you for Your supernatural power and amazing administration in and over our lives. Order our steps this day and go before us to make the crooked places straight. Thank you for protection throughout this day both on land and in the air. Thank you for miracles, signs, and wonders. Thank you for health, healing, and wholeness. Be glorified this day and use us for Your glory. Bless my family and friends and meet their needs. Thank you, Lord! In Jesus' mighty name. Amen.

Posted on Facebook August 12, 2014

Father God, thank you for this new day that You have made. We rejoice and am grateful and glad in it. Thank you for health, healing, and soundness of mind. There is no one greater than You. You are awesome and amazing and we thank you for new mercy and grace.

I plead the blood of Jesus over our schools and pray for a safe, productive, favor-filled school year. I pray our children have good success in every subject and God-ordained teachers/staff. They are diligent and studious. Remove anyone with evil intent.

Thank you, Lord, for peace and protection in and over every day. You are faithful. Minister to the needs of every family. Use me for Your glory.

Demonstrate Your power and be glorified in the lives of Your people. Save, heal, comfort, encourage, strengthen and provide. In Jesus' mighty name. Amen.

Father God, thank you for a sound, well-balanced mind and a soul and life surrendered to You. Help me to be who You've called me to be. Thank you, Lord, for salvation and success that can only be found in your Son Jesus. Use me for Your glory. In Jesus' name, amen.

Father God, thank you for this new day that You have made. It is a blessed day of victory because we are breathing. We enter Your gates with thanks giving and Your courts with praise. We overcome because You are greater than any and every situation and circumstance and with You living inside of us we have the power to overcome. You are our Helper, our Strong Tower, and our Refuge. You are our Hope, our Security, and our Salvation.

I lift up to You all those in need right now. I pray for divine intervention. I pray for peace of mind and salvation to the lost and hopeless. I pray for Your light to invade the darkness of depression, discouragement, and oppression. I pray for Your peace to quiet torment, confusion, and frustration. I pray for provision for those in lack. I pray for open doors of opportunity, employment and promotion without opposition. I pray for healing in bodies and minds. I pray for comfort for those experiencing a loss or expecting a death.

Father, I come against demonic activity and demonic influence. I come against the spirit of suicide and premature death. I plead the life-saving blood of Jesus over our schools, workplaces, neighborhoods and communities. I pray for peace and calm where there is unrest. I pray for protection going out and coming in. I pray for justice to be done. Thank you for satisfying us with long life and showing us Your salvation.

Demonstrate Your power in and through the lives of your people. Use us for Your glory. I pray Your people called by Your name shall humble ourselves, pray, seek Your face and turn from our wicked ways. You promise to then hear from heaven, forgive our sin and heal our land. Our land needs healing. Thank you, Lord.

I pray that everyone not in their set place would submit to Your plan and purpose. I pray for forgiveness and restoration. I pray for healing and reconciliation. I pray for order and Divine alignment. I pray for resources for every God-ordained assignment. Father, be glorified this day.

Thank you, Lord. In Jesus' mighty name I pray with thanksgiving. Amen.

Posted on Facebook August 15, 2014

Father God, thank you for this new and blessed day that You have made. Thank you for health, healing, and wholeness. Thank you for forgiveness, favor and Your faithfulness. We trust You because You promise never to leave or forsake us. We trust You because You are greater than anything and anyone that we face. We trust You because we have the victory and always win in Christ Jesus. We are not moved by what we see or hear but only by what we believe. We believe the report of The Lord. Have Your way in our lives. In Jesus' name. Amen.

Posted on Facebook August 18, 2014

Father God, thank you for this new day that You have made. I rejoice. I am grateful and glad. You are faithful. There is no one like You. There is no one greater than You.

Thank you for Your continued protection over our lives. I lift up our schools and universities and plead the blood of Jesus over every campus, building, classroom and playground. Thank you for uncovering the plan in Santa Clarita. If it was not real, reveal to that youngster the ignorance in making such a joke. I come against all demonic activity and influence for destruction. I pray for Your people to stand for righteousness and holiness and to stand in the gap between life and death. I pray for a safe environment where our students can succeed. Uncover teachers and staff who are perverted and being used by the enemy to hurt the children they are to protect.

Father, may our children have a healthy environment both at home and school in which to learn. Thank you for safety wherever they go. Help them to make right, godly choices. I pray for a safe, successful school year.

Thank you, Lord. In Jesus' name. Amen. Have a blessed, peaceful and productive week!

Posted on Facebook August 20, 2014

Father God, our land needs peace and that peace can only be found in You. I pray for all those in position of authority in whatever capacity for wisdom, understanding and godly counsel. I plead the blood of Jesus over our person and property for protection from demonic interactions and those who have ill intent. I pray for healing in our land. I pray for revival and return to righteousness. I pray that Your people called by Your name shall be humble, pray, seek Your face and turn from wickedness so that You may hear from heaven, forgive our sin and heal our land. Demonstrate Your power, Lord. In Jesus' name. Amen.

Posted on Facebook August 21, 2014

This is the day that The Lord has made. I rejoice and am glad in it. Father God, I lift up everyone on my friend's list to You whether in the VI, Maryland, Pennsylvania or California; from Wesleyan, Eudora Kean or Morgan; from Huber, LPCC or HCASC; and family by birth or marriage, friend, colleague or acquaintance.

I pray for their needs to be met whether for salvation, healing, provision, protection or promotion; for peace, joy, hope, strength or encouragement. Demonstrate Your power in the lives of Your people. I pray for miracles, signs, and wonders. I pray for breakthrough, turnaround, sudden change and restoration. You are faithful and can be trusted. Thy will be done this day. Thank you, Lord! In Jesus' mighty name. Amen!

Posted on Facebook August 22, 2014

Father God, thank you for this new, blessed day of breakthrough, turnaround, sudden change and victory that You have made. I rejoice, and I am glad.

Thank you for wisdom, revelation, insight, understanding and discernment. Thank you for health, healing, and wholeness. Thank you for a sound, well-balanced mind. Thank you for satisfying me with long, abundant life and showing me Your salvation.

Thank you for peace, protection, provision, promotion and prosperity. Thank you for fulfillment and manifestation of purpose and destiny. I come against distractions and all demonic activity that will try to hinder destiny. I thank you that the enemy is already defeated and Your plans for me will prosper. You are faithful, and I trust You.

Be glorified in my life this day. Demonstrate Your power on my behalf this day. Thank you for open doors of favor. Thy will be done. Thank you, Lord. In Jesus' mighty name. Amen.

Posted on Facebook August 24, 2014

Father God, I lift up the Meadow family and Morgan community especially the athletics department and pray for comfort and peace that passes all human understanding. Meet their needs and heal the pain caused by this sudden death. Thank you, Lord. You are faithful. In Jesus' mighty name, Amen.

Posted on Facebook August 24, 2014

Father God, I lift up my niece and her roommates as they start their junior year tomorrow, my godson as he starts his senior year and the entire student body, faculty, staff, and administration of Morgan State University as well as all other schools resuming tomorrow. I pray the blood of Jesus covers every campus. I pray for safety going out and coming in. I pray for wisdom, understanding and good success in the classroom. I pray a hedge of protection from the forces of darkness. Thank you, Father. In Jesus' name. Amen.

Posted on Facebook August 25, 2014

Father God, comfort the family members and friends of Antonio Smith, Michael Brown and all whose lives have been snuffed out all too soon. I plead the blood of Jesus over the city of Chicago and pray for an end to the senseless violence. Break up the gangs. Uncover and arrest all the suspects in every killing. I come against premature death. Heal that land. In Jesus' name, amen.

Posted on Facebook August 26, 2014

Father God, thank you for this new day that You have made. Thank you for supernatural strength to endure in this season. Thank you for favor and grace to succeed in this season.

Thank you for divine connections, partners and prayer warriors to support my assignment in this season. Thank you for miracles, signs, and wonders in this season. Thank you for peace, protection, provision and promotion in this season.

Thank you for never leaving or forsaking me in this season. Thank you for breakthrough, turnaround and sudden change in this season. Thank you for victory in this season.

Father, You are faithful, and I trust You. Thank you for satisfying me with long, abundant, healthy life and a sound, well-balanced mind and showing me Your salvation. Demonstrate Your power in the lives of Your people. Strengthen, encourage and energize those who may feel like giving up.

You prepared our comeback before the attack, so we will not breakdown, give up, give in, or give out. We praise You, honor You and give You all the glory. Thank you, Lord. In Jesus' mighty name. Amen.

Posted on Facebook August 28, 2014

Father God, thank you for this new day that You have made. I rejoice and am glad in it. I love you Lord. I choose not to be anxious because You have everything under control. Nothing surprises You. I praise You God for You are faithful. I thank you for never leaving or forsaking me. I trust You for the victory. I am healed by the stripes Jesus bore and live to declare the mighty works of The Lord. Be glorified in and through my life. Order my steps.

Minister to the needs of those of my FB friends. Save, heal, comfort, encourage, protect, promote, elevate, deliver, restore, provide for and strengthen. There is no one greater than You. You are worthy Lord. You are awesome and amazing. You are majestic and mighty. Thank you for forgiveness, mercy, and grace. Great is Your faithfulness. Thank you for salvation and eternal security. In Jesus' mighty name with Thanksgiving, I pray. Amen. Have a peaceful and productive day!

Posted on Facebook August 28, 2014

Father God, I lift up Joan Rivers to You and pray for mercy and grace. I pray for salvation and that she would receive You as Savior and Lord if she hasn't already accepted Your Son, Jesus. I pray for accurate diagnosis and treatment. Heal Jehovah Rapha. Thank you, Lord. In Jesus' name. Amen.

Posted on Facebook August 31, 2014

Father God, I thank you for a sound, well-balanced mind. I lift up those challenged with Alzheimer's and dementia and pray for healing and turnaround.

Restore like only You can. Thank you, Lord. In Jesus' name. Amen.

Posted on Facebook Wednesday, September 3, 2014

Father God, thank you for this new day that You have made. Thank you for health, strength, and turnaround in both. Thank you for healing and wholeness manifested in every organ. Thank you for peace throughout this day. Thank you for freedom to worship You. Thank you for mercy and grace.

Heal our land, Lord. Save souls. Change lives. Deliver minds. Heal bodies. Blessed is the nation whose God is The Lord. May we stand for righteousness and holiness and return to being one nation under God. You are faithful and forgiving. Minister to my family members and FB friends and my Pastors and church family. Order our steps and orchestrate our day. Protect our going out and coming in. Be glorified in our lives.

Thank you, Lord. In Jesus' mighty name. Amen. Have a great day! Happy Wednesday!

Posted on Facebook September 4, 2014

Father God, You are faithful, and I trust You. I pray for sound, sweet sleep that I may wake rested and refreshed in the morning. I know the thoughts and plans that You have for me. They are thoughts and plans for welfare and peace and not for evil, to give me hope for my final outcome. Thank you, Lord. In Jesus' name. Amen.

Posted on Facebook September 5, 2014

Thank you, President David Wilson! Father God, cover this fine institution founded in 1867 as the Centenary Biblical Institute. I pray that the administration, faculty, staff and alumni would all serve in the best interest of the students and the university. Protect and provide for the needs. May honesty and integrity govern every action. Thank you, Lord, for Fair Morgan. In Jesus' name. Amen.

Posted on Facebook September 8, 2014

Dear Heavenly Father, thank you for this new day that You have made. Thank you for loving us and never leaving or forsaking us. Thank you for provision of eternal security through the shed blood of Your Son Jesus. Thank you for the ministry of the Holy Spirit, our Comforter, Teacher, and Guide. You are omnipresent, omniscient and omnipotent. There is no one greater than You. You are worthy of all honor, glory, and praise. You are faithful and can be trusted. You are forgiving, and we thank you for brand new mercies.

I lift up my family members, FB friends, associates, acquaintances and church family (past and present) to You right now. I also lift up the United States of America. I pray for salvation for those who have never accepted Jesus as Savior and Lord. I pray for rededication for those who have grown cold or have been deceived in their relationship and fellowship with You. I pray for restoration and healing to take place in minds, bodies, families, homes, churches and wherever change is needed. I pray for Your people, called by Your name, to humble ourselves, pray, seek Your face and turn from our wicked ways. You promise to then hear from heaven, forgive our sin and heal our land.

Father God, I pray for protection as we go out and come in. I pray for peace to surround us and saturate our environment. I pray for honesty and integrity to govern our lives and decision making. I pray for provision for basic needs, dreams, and visions. I pray for open doors without opposition. I pray Your perfect will be done in and through the lives of Your people.

I come against deception, discouragement, depression and oppression. I come against confusion, frustration, and irritation that would delay Kingdom building and progress and fulfillment of God-ordained destiny. Show Yourself strong on behalf of Your people this day, week and month. I pray for victory, turnaround and sudden change.

I pray for faith in You to be strengthened and built up. I pray that You get the glory from our lives. I thank you for the testimony that is coming from our time of testing. Restore, save, heal, transform, renew, comfort, strengthen, encourage, deliver, provide for, promote, elevate, activate and anoint those in need. God, You are faithful, and I trust You.

I plead the blood of Jesus over our schools and children. Cover them from evil and demonic influences and activity. Help them excel in the classroom and everything constructive they do. Lord, stir up the gifts in them and us. May we accept and complete the assignment You have called us to do. Be glorified in our lives. Order our steps this day, week and month. Thank you, Lord. In Jesus' mighty name. Amen. Have a wonderful week!

Posted on Facebook September 8, 2014

Father, thank you for satisfying S. Truett Cathy with long life and showing him Your salvation. May his legacy and commitment to godly principles and convictions continue. I pray for comfort for his family, friends, and company. I pray for souls to be saved as his life is celebrated. Encourage and strengthen all those who knew and loved him. Be glorified. Thank you, Lord. In Jesus' name. Amen.

Posted on Facebook September 8, 2014

God's timing is so perfect. I bought the book, Joy Comes in the Morning by Shelia B. Scott, in September 2011 in support of the author. God had a different plan. It got placed in a bag with other books and papers only to be pulled out a few weeks ago. I started reading it and was so encouraged by it I kept going and just finished it. I called the author earlier this evening to express appreciation for saying yes to God to share her testimony. My last couple months have been one of great testing. God is faithful, so I am excited and in expectation that I will walk through this victoriously. God is my Healer, my Deliverer, my Strength, my Protection, my Peace, my Joy, my Provider, my Sustainer, my Guide, my Teacher, my Helper, my Keeper, my Restorer, my Refuge, my All.

Posted on Facebook September 11, 2014

I was working in Baltimore, MD at Huber Memorial Church when our country, our world, our lives, as we knew it, would forever change. Everyone has been impacted.

Father God, thank you for this new day that You have made. Thank you for brand new mercy. Thank you for peace and strength that is only found in You. Thank you for protection, provision, and promotion in every area. Thank you for safety and eternal security available through the finished work of the shed blood of Your Son and my Savior Jesus Christ.

I pray for rededication, revival and return to righteousness. I pray for surrender and submission to godly, biblical principles. I pray for healing in our land.

Thank you, Lord, for good success. Thank you, Lord, for never leaving or forsaking us. Thank you for blessing our going out and coming in. Order our steps. Demonstrate Your power in and through the lives of Your people. In Jesus' mighty name. Amen.

Posted on Facebook September 11, 2014

Father God, I lift up everyone who lost a loved one on 9/11/01 in the attacks that took place that day. I lift up everyone who have lost a loved one since through serving this country because of those attacks. Comfort, strengthen and encourage hearts and minds. Heal those living with hurt and constant reminders. I pray for peace. Thank you, Lord! In Jesus' name. Amen.

Posted on Facebook September 12, 2014

Father God, thank you for continued healing. You are faithful, and I trust You. Thank you for strength to get through the week. Thank you for sweet sleep and sound rest. Grateful for peace. In Jesus' name. Amen. Have a wonderful weekend!

Posted on Facebook September 16, 2014

Father God, You are not moved, troubled or perplexed by what is taking place in our lives, homes, communities, and country. And because You are at peace, I rest in the confidence that You are causing all things to work for my/ our good and Your glory. You are greater than anything and anyone coming against me/us. You are more powerful than any and every challenge I/we face. I/we will continue to stand.

Though at times, there may be moments of weariness and discouragement, I know I am victorious and shall walk through this as Your living testimony/ Your witness. I have destiny and purpose to fulfill. I shall declare the mighty works of The Lord. Thank you for never leaving me or forsaking me.

I lift up everyone going through a challenge right now. I pray for healing, Supernatural physical and mental strength, peace, joy, hope, salvation, deliverance, breakthrough, turnaround, sudden change, restoration, provision, favor, open doors without opposition, miracles, signs, and wonders. Demonstrate Your power. Show Yourself strong. Be glorified. Thank you for the victory that is already ours through Christ Jesus. You are faithful. I trust You. In Jesus' mighty and matchless name, amen.

Posted on Facebook September 16, 2014

Father God, I plead the blood of Jesus over the entire Morgan State University campus including Morgan View Apartments and pray for protection from vandalism, accident, incident, and foolishness. I pray a hedge of protection as the students, faculty, and staff go and come. I come against demonic activity and influence and pray for Your presence to rest, rule, reign, abide over and saturate everything and everyone connected to Morgan State. I pray for good success in the classroom, offices and athletic venues. I pray Your will be done. Thank you that all is well with that fire incident. Rest and relax my niece, her roommates and everyone residing at Morgan View. Thank you, Lord. In Jesus' mighty name. Amen. Going to sleep because You neither slumber nor sleep.

Posted on Facebook September 21, 2014

I decree and declare peace and order over this day! Hallelujah! Thank you, Lord! Father God, You are not the author of confusion. I thank you for this blessed day of victory that You have made. In Jesus' name. Amen.

Posted on Facebook September 24, 2014

Father God, I thank you for this new, blessed day of victory that You have made. Thank you for protection, provision, promotion, and peace. Thank you for health, strength and a sound, well-balanced mind. Thank you for Your plans for me, plans for peace and not for evil and plans to give me an expected end. Thank you for breakthrough, turnaround and sudden change.

I lift up my family members and FB friends, my pastors and church family and pray Your will be done. Heal, save, deliver, protect, encourage, comfort, strengthen, guide, restore and provide for those in need. I pray for open doors without opposition.

Be glorified in the lives of Your people. Show Yourself strong on behalf of your people. Demonstrate Your power through Your people. You are faithful. I trust You. In Jesus' name. Amen. Have a wonderful Wednesday FB friends!

Posted on Facebook September 26, 2014

Father God, thank you for this blessed day that You have made. I call this day and weekend blessed. You are causing all things to work for my good and Your glory. You are restoring and healing and perfecting everything concerning me. Thank you that no weapon formed against my family or me shall prosper.

I praise You because I am fearfully and wonderfully made. Use me for Your glory! Order my steps and orchestrate my assignment.

Demonstrate Your mighty power on my behalf. You are faithful and I will forever trust You.

Thank you for favor, promotion, breakthrough, turnaround, sudden change and VICTORY! I lift up my family members and friends and pray for their needs to be met. Thank you, Lord! In Jesus' name. Amen. Have a fantastic Friday and wonderful weekend family!

Posted on Facebook September 29, 2014

Father God, thank you that no weapon formed against me, my family members, my fitness, my finances or my future shall prosper. I will bless The Lord at all times. His praise shall continually be in my mouth.

Posted on Facebook October 1, 2014

Father God, thank you for this new day and new month that You have made. It's a blessed day and month of victory. You have graced us for every assignment and for whatever You allow to come into our life.

We will not faint or grow weary, but we will pray without ceasing and stay in faith. We will press. We will trust You. We will finish the year strong. We will not be distracted, discouraged or depressed by the fiery darts/lies of the enemy.

We thank you that no weapon formed against us shall prosper. We thank you that greater are You who resides within us than he who resides in this world. We thank you for never leaving or forsaking us.

Order my steps and orchestrate my activities that I may fulfill Your assignment for my life. Bless my family, friends, coworkers, pastors, church family and FB friends. You know the needs. Save, heal, comfort, encourage, deliver, provide for, strengthen and protect.

Cover our homes, schools, places of employment, churches and wherever we go from the demonic influences and activities of the evil one. I pray a hedge of protection and plead the blood of Jesus over our children. May we hunger and thirst after righteousness and holiness. Guide us Holy Spirit. Thank you,

Lord, for Your mercy and grace, love, and forgiveness. In Jesus' mighty name. Amen. Happy Wednesday!

Prayer Covering Text to my family Thursday, October 2, 2014

Father God, thank you for this blessed day of victory that You have made. By Jesus' stripes, we are healed, so I thank you for physical, mental, spiritual, emotional and relational wholeness. Thank you for a sound, well-balanced mind. You are Jehovah Jireh. You provide for every need. I pray for total surrender to Your plan and purpose for our lives. I plead the blood of Jesus over my family. No weapon formed against us shall prosper. I pray for a hunger and thirst after righteousness. I pray for breakthrough, turnaround and sudden change. I pray for protection and come against premature death. I come against demonic activity, interaction, and assignments that try to hinder destiny. Thank you for good success in every area. I pray for salvation, rededication, and commitment to You. Use us for Your glory and order our steps. Thank you, Lord. In Jesus' name. Amen.

Posted on Facebook Monday, October 6, 2014

Father God, thank you for this new, blessed day that You have made. I walk in victory, overflow, and increase in every area because of what Jesus did on Calvary. Thank you for forgiveness, mercy, and grace. Great is Your faithfulness. I plead the blood of Jesus over every family member. Thank you for health, healing, and wholeness and satisfying us with long life and showing us Your salvation. I come against every demonic plan, plot and ploy to hinder our purpose and destiny. I come against confusion, frustration, discouragement and distraction from my God-given assignment. Lord, I love You and thank You for this day of breakthrough, turnaround and sudden change. Thank you, Holy Spirit for wisdom, discernment, and understanding. Thank you for vision and provision. Thank you for protection and peace. Thank you for favor.

Father God, bless, save, heal, deliver, encourage, comfort, strengthen and provide for those in need. I pray a hedge of protection around our schools, our workplaces, and our communities. Reveal and remove anything and anyone not of you. Demonstrate Your power, Lord. I come against accident, injury and premature death. Thank you for good success this day and week. You are faithful and can be trusted. In Jesus' mighty name. Amen. Have an amazing, blessed week!

Posted on Facebook October 7, 2014

Hallelujah! This is the day that The Lord has made. I will rejoice and be glad in it. Thank you, Father, for this blessed day of victory and favor. Thank you for brand new mercies. Thank you for health, healing and wholeness in every area of my life and my family member's lives. Thank you for a hedge of protection around everyone and everything connected to me. Thank you for satisfying us with long life and showing us Your salvation. In Jesus' mighty name. Amen. Have an amazing day FB friends!

Posted on Facebook October 8, 2014

Living Praise Christian Center family and friends, remain focused on Christ and let's not be moved by what we see or hear. God is faithful and can be trusted.

Father God, thank you for this blessed day, week and month of victory in the lives of our Pastors, church family, staff, volunteers, leaders, and partners. We win in every area. We are in expectation for prayers to be answered. We decree and declare peace, order, and productivity and come against all distractions and hindrances to our destiny and assignment. We thank you for protection, provision, and promotion. We thank you for open doors without opposition. In Jesus' mighty name. Amen.

Posted on Facebook Thursday, October 9, 2014

(Motivated by last night's Bible study teaching and tonight's Biggest Loser) I am who God says I am. I can do what God says I can do. I have what God says I have. I am healed. I am whole. I am confident. I am a champion. I am a finisher. I am blessed. I am anointed. I am above. I am the head. I am chosen. I am equipped. I am diligent. I am disciplined. I am motivated. I am strong. I am debt free. I am God's distribution channel. I am a leader. I am focused. I am an encourager. I am a prayer warrior. I am a threat to the enemy. I am victorious. I am a visionary. My confidence is in Christ. My security and salvation are in the shed blood of Jesus and His finished work on the cross.

Posted on Facebook October 11, 2014

Father God, thank you for blessing our mom with another year of life. Continue to satisfy her with long, healthy, abundant life and show her Your salvation. In Jesus' name. Amen.

Text to Hubby October 15, 2014

Father God, thank you for this new day with brand new mercy. Great is Your faithfulness. Thank you for Robert and our blessed relationship. Order our steps and guide our actions, Holy Spirit. Cover and protect our going out and coming in. I plead the blood of Jesus over Jennifer and Maya. As for me and my house, we shall serve The Lord. Forgive us of our sins in word, thought or deed. Help us to be who You've called us to be. Thank you for favor, provision, and promotion wherever we go. Use us for Your glory. Thank you for complete healing. Minister to our family members. Save, Heal, Deliver, Comfort, Encourage, and Provide. I come against backlash and jealousy to Robert's success in the workplace. Shine through him. Father, thank you. In Jesus' name. Amen.

Posted on Facebook October 18, 2014

Father God, thank you for this new, blessed day of victory that You have made. Order my steps over this wonderful weekend. Holy Spirit, lead and guide me. Thank you for forgiveness and favor. Thank you for peace, protection, promotion and prosperity. I am Your distribution channel. Use me for Your glory. I am staying in faith and finishing strong. Bless my family, friends, pastors, church family and my alma mater. Thank you, Lord! In Jesus' mighty name. Amen. Be safe and enjoy!

Posted on Facebook October 20, 2014

Father God, I lift up Tasha Harvey-Alexander, Tanya Harvey, and their entire family to You on the passing of Mr. Harvey. Minister healing like only You can. Comfort them and saturate them in Your peace that passes all understanding. I come against guilt and regret. As they prepare to celebrate his life, meet every need. You promise never to leave or forsake us so may they feel You near walking with them every step of the way.

Thank you for hearing and answering. In Jesus' name. Amen. Your LPCC family loves you, and we're here for you.

Posted on Facebook Monday, October 20, 2014, 10:45 pm

Father God, thank you for family whether by birth, marriage, friendship or fellowship. Help us to love one another as You would have us to love. Restore and repair any broken relationships. Save those who don't know You as Savior and Lord. Heal those who walked away because of offense, disappointment, discouragement, deception or error. Where a door was left open for the enemy to come in, we pray for turn-around and correction. Deliver those in darkness. You wish that none would perish, so we lift up every family member to You. We call them into the Kingdom of Heaven.

I lift up every person experiencing the loss of a loved one right now. Heal hearts and hurts. Meet needs. Workout schedules. Comfort, strengthen and encourage. I pray for supernatural mental, emotional and physical strength and stamina to go through the process. Provide rest for the weary. Ease the pain. God, You are faithful and can be trusted. Thank you, Lord. In Jesus' name. Amen.

Posted on Facebook Thursday, October 23, 2014, 11:25 pm

Dear Heavenly Father, hallowed be Your Holy name. I thank and praise You for this blessed day You saw us through. Thank you for your care and compassion. Thank you for your love, joy, and peace. Thank you for never leaving us or forsaking us. Thank you for protection and provision. Thank you for forgiveness and favor. Thank you for mercy and grace.

I lift up everyone who has lost a loved one recently or not so recent. I pray for comfort and strength whether it was sudden or expected. I pray for peace and encouragement to continue to live. I pray for hearts to be healed. I pray for needs to be met. I come against guilt and regret. Saturate them with Your love.

Father, I lift up everyone going through a challenge whether physical, mental, emotional, relational, marital or financial. I pray for healing, breakthrough, and turnaround. You are yet performing miracles. You are Jehovah Rapha, and I know You to be my Healer. I plead the blood of

Jesus over every situation, circumstance, and negative report and pray for You to cause a shift in the diagnosis, report, and relationship.

Lord, I lift up every caregiver. Give them Supernatural physical and mental strength to provide the needed care. Replenish and restore everything they give out. Send help to lighten the load. Provide resources to ease the expense.

Father, I lift up everyone who will see this post and pray for their needs to be met. Save, heal, deliver, comfort, encourage, strengthen, provide for, protect, promote, increase, elevate, restore. God, You are faithful and more than able.

Bless my family and Facebook friends, my pastors and church family. Cover our schools, neighborhoods, and communities. Reveal and remove anything and anyone not a part of Your plan for our lives. Help us to remain fixed and focused on our assignment. Use us for Your glory and demonstrate Your power in our lives. Show Yourself strong on our behalf and grant us the desires of our heart as we delight in You. We surrender all to You. We trust You. We submit to Your will and way for our lives. Thank you, Lord! In Jesus' mighty name, amen. Have a blessed day and weekend of victory!

Text to Hubby Monday, October 27, 2014 (Cover your mate)

Father God, thank you for this blessed day that You have made. Thank you for victory in every situation because all things work for our good and Your glory. Thank you for open doors of opportunity, employment, promotion and increase without opposition and for wisdom and discernment to manage these opportunities well. I plead the blood of Jesus over our homes, schools, and workplaces. I come against demonic activity and distractions that would try to hinder our destiny and assignment. I pray that You saturate his/her workplace and mine with Your presence. I pray for salvation and deliverance where needed. God, give us direction concerning when and where to move. We are finishers, so we will continue to stand in Your power and strength. We will not get weary and faint, but we will pray and wage war against the enemy. We are victorious for greater is You in us than he who is in this world.

We love and trust You. Thank you, Lord! In Jesus' powerful and mighty name. Amen.

Father God, we dwell in Your secret place. We thank you for being our Refuge and our Fortress. On You, we lean and rely, and in You, we confidently trust! You deliver us from the snare of the fowler and from the deadly pestilence. You cover us with Your feathers, and under Your wings shall we trust and find refuge; Your truth and Your faithfulness are a shield and a buckler. We shall not be afraid of the terror of the night, nor of the arrow (the evil plots and slanders of the wicked) that flies by day, nor of the pestilence that stalks in darkness, nor of the destruction and sudden death that surprise and lay waste at noonday. A thousand may fall at our side, and ten thousand at our right hand, but it shall not come near us. Only a spectator shall we be inaccessible in the secret place of the Most High as we witness there ward of the wicked. Because we have made the Lord our refuge, and the Most High our dwelling place, there shall no evil befall us, nor any plague or calamity come near our tent. For You will give Your angels charge over us to accompany and defend and preserve us in all our ways (of obedience and service). They shall bear us up on their hands, lest we dash our foot against a stone. We shall tread upon the lion and adder; the young lion and the serpent shall we trample underfoot. Because we have set our love upon You, therefore will You deliver us; You will set us on high, because we know and understand Your name. We have a personal knowledge of Your mercy, love, and kindness, trust, and rely on You, knowing You will never forsake us, no, never. We shall call upon You, and You will answer us; You will be with us in trouble, You will deliver us and honor us. With long life will You satisfy us and show us Your salvation. Thank you that no weapon formed against us shall prosper. Thank you that sickness, disease, and a virus cannot stay in our bodies. Thank you for protection, provision, promotion, and peace. Thank you for this blessed day of victory that You have made. Thank you, Lord. In Jesus' name. Amen (Psalm 91, AMP)

Posted on Facebook October 30, 2014

Father God, thank you for this blessed day of victory that You have made. Thank you for brand new mercies. Great is Your faithfulness. I decree and declare peace, order, productivity and favor over this day. Thank you for protection and provision. Thank you for promotion and elevation. Thank you for breakthrough, turnaround and sudden change. Move in the lives of Your people. Demonstrate Your power and show Yourself strong. I thank you that my family, fitness, finances and future are all blessed. I thank you that no weapon formed shall prosper and You cause all things to work together for our good and Your glory. Thank you for health, healing, and wholeness. Thank you, Lord. In Jesus' name. Amen.

Posted on Facebook October 31, 2014

Father God, there is no one like You. There is no one greater than You. This is the day that You Lord have made. I rejoice. I am grateful and glad.

Thank you for victory in this day. Thank you that no weapon formed against us shall prosper for we trust You. I plead the blood of Jesus over our home, schools, neighborhoods and work places. I come against confusion, frustration, foolishness and all demonic activity and interference.

I decree peace and order over our entire day. I thank you for protection from dangers seen and unseen. May Your light shine through us bringing illumination to every dark place. I pray a hedge around our children. I come against premature death.

Order our steps. Be glorified in our lives. Demonstrate Your power. Uncover the plans of the enemy. Thank you for wisdom, insight, and discernment. Thank you for knowledge and understanding.

I lift up my family and FB friends. Bless, save, heal, comfort, restore, rescue, deliver, strengthen, encourage, protect, provide for every need. Thank you, Lord, for this blessed day that You have made. Thank you for going before us to make the crooked places straight. I love You. Lord. In Jesus' powerful and mighty name. Amen. Have a great day!

Posted on Facebook November 10, 2014

Father God, as the Myles Munroe Leadership Conference continues to minister to the lives of everyone involved. Speak to and through every presenter. I come against fear and pray for power, love and soundness of mind to saturate this gathering. Demonstrate Your power. I pray for hearts and minds to be focused on You. Heal, comfort, encourage and strengthen. Thank you, Father. In Jesus' mighty name. Amen.

Posted on Facebook November 10, 2014

Father God, thank you for this blessed day of victory that You have made. I thank you for peace and productivity throughout this day. Thank you for protection and provision in this day. I come against distractions from purpose. Thank you for health, healing and wholeness in every area of our lives. Bless my family, friends, church family and the Body of Christ this day. Thank you, Lord! You are faithful. We honor and adore You. We love You, Lord. We bless Your name and magnify Your Word. In Jesus' mighty name. Amen. Happy Blessed Monday!

Posted on Facebook Tuesday, November 11, 2014

Father God, thank you for this blessed day of victory that You have made. As we honor and recognize our veterans this day, I thank you for all who served and continue to serve. I thank you for my dad and other family members and friends who served and continue to do so. I lift up the family members who served alongside them. I pray that this country would properly honor our veterans. I pray for basic needs to be met. I pray we don't return to business, as usual, tomorrow but that we seek out ways to rightly recognize our military personnel. I pray a covering over our Armed Forces and a hedge of protection around them. Heal PTSD and every other mental, physical and emotional injury and impact. Thank you, Lord. You are faithful. In Jesus' mighty and matchless name. Amen!

Posted on Facebook November 14, 2014

Dear Heavenly Father, thank you for this blessed day of victory that You have made. Thank you for going before us to make the crooked places straight. Thank you for protection in our going out and coming in. Thank you for peace over our day. Thank you for provision for purpose. Thank you for health, healing and wholeness in every area of our lives. Thank you for promotion, increase and elevation. Thank you for strength to carry out our assignment. Thank you for focus. Bless our family members and friends this day. We love You and Thank you, Lord. In Jesus' name. Amen.

Text to Hubby Monday, November 17, 2014

Father, thank you for this blessed, productive day of victory. Thank you that all things work together for our good and Your glory. Thank you for wisdom, insight and understanding to walk in excellence in every area and assignment. Thank you for favor with whoever we encounter. We come against backlash and demonic activity and interference. Thank you, Lord. In Jesus' name. Amen.

Posted on Facebook Wednesday, November 19, 2014

Father God, thank you for this new and blessed day of victory that You have made. Thank you for brand new mercies this day. Great is Your faithfulness. Thank you for provision and protection as we go forth on our assignment this day moving in the purpose You have for our lives. I declare peace, order and productivity over this day. Thank you for favor with those we encounter.

I lift up my family members and FB friends, my Pastors and church family and pray Your will be done. Bless, heal, save, rescue, deliver, comfort, encourage, strengthen and provide for every need. Demonstrate Your power. Show Yourself strong on our behalf. Use us for Your glory. Thank you, Lord. In Jesus' mighty name, amen.

Text to Hubby Wednesday, November 19, 2014, 7:00 am

Father God, I lift up Robert to You right now. I thank you for his partnership, leadership and support. I thank you for unity in our marriage. I thank you for turnaround, healing and restoration in our lives. I thank you for favor. I thank you for wisdom, insight and understanding. Thank you for financial debt freedom. Thank you for overflow and increase. Thank you for open doors of opportunity, employment and promotion without opposition. Have Your way. Use us for Your glory. In Jesus' name. Amen.

Father God, I lift up my Julia, Britt, Cee and even Leilani to You. I thank you for turnaround, healing and restoration. I thank you for favor and good success and wisdom, insight and understanding. Thank you for financial debt freedom. Thank you for overflow and increase. Have Your way. Be glorified. In Jesus' name. Amen.

Father God, I lift up my sister and friend to You and pray that all is well in her fitness, family and finances. I speak peace and order in her midst and come against frustration, irritation and all distractions to her destiny. I pray for balance in every area and favor in her workplace. Minister mental, emotional and physical strength, healing and wholeness to her now. Thank you for Your faithful servant. In Jesus' name. Amen.

Posted on Facebook Friday, November 21, 2014

Father God, thank you for this blessed day of victory and favor. Thank you for health, healing and wholeness. Thank you for protection and provision. Thank you for turnaround, breakthrough and sudden change. Thank you for forgiveness, salvation and restoration. Thank you for comfort and encouragement. We are not moved by what we see, hear or feel. We trust You. We are victorious, and our confidence is in Christ. Thank you, Lord! In Jesus' mighty name. Amen. Have a dynamic day Facebook friends!

Father God, thank you for our teens. I lift up the leaders of RockNow and pray You impart wisdom and insight to be able to minister to and reach where parents/guardians can't/don't. Bless the households of every teen from every campus. Thank you for our Pastors and bless them for their time and investment into the lives of this generation. Father, we will not lose one child to the enemy. We decree and declare that each one will live to declare the mighty works of the Lord and fulfill their God-ordained destiny. They will be change agents in their schools and community. Bless everyone who helped to Amen.

Posted on Facebook November 27, 2014

Father God, thank you for this new day and new opportunity to say thank you. Thank you for safe travels Thank you for the fellowship of family and friends. Rest us as we sleep especially Robert who did all the driving.

Thank you for protection and provision for every need. Thank you for eternal security. Bless my family and friends. Bless the LPCC Thanksgiving outreach and everyone cooking, serving or participating in any way. Minister to the needs of everyone attending.

Thank you for this weekend of refreshing, restoration and healing. You are faithful and can be trusted. There is no one greater than You. There is no one like You Lord. You are worthy of all our praise and honor. In Jesus' name. Amen!

Happy Blessed Thanksgiving Day!

Posted on Facebook Saturday, November 29, 2014, 11:55 pm

Father God, thank you for Your hand in and over my life. You are so faithful. Thank you for a wonderful weekend of relaxation and restoration fellowshipping with family. Thank you for protection and provision.

Your plans for me are for good and not for evil. Your plans are to give me an expected end. I pray for wisdom, insight and discernment. Pray for courage and boldness to go forth in the assignment You have for my life.

I thank you that no weapon formed against my family or me shall prosper. I declare as for me and my house we shall serve the Lord. I thank you for victory in every area. I thank you that You cause all things to work together for my good because I love You and are called according to Your purpose.

I thank you for breakthrough, turnaround and sudden change on behalf of my family members and friends in need. We are not moved by what we see, hear or feel. We are moved only by what we believe, and we believe Your Word is true. We believe the report of the Lord. We believe what You say about us.

We shall not back down, give up, give in or give out. We shall press on, pray without ceasing and take new territory. We shall not get weary in well-doing. We shall remain on the front line knowing the battle is not ours, but it belongs to the Lord.

I declare we win. I come against confusion, distractions, demonic interference and premature death. I plead the blood of Jesus over myself, my family, my friends, my pastors and church family and declare that we shall live and declare the mighty works of the Lord.

We shall finish this year strong. We shall remain focused on the goal. Thank you, Lord, for supernatural strength. Thank you for health, healing and wholeness. I pray for salvation for the lost. I pray for deliverance for those who are bound. I pray for comfort for the grieving and encouragement for the depressed and discouraged. Minister to the needs of those reading this prayer. Demonstrate Your power and show Yourself strong on behalf of Your people.

Father, I trust You. I give You all the praise, honor and glory. Thank you, Lord, for this new day. In Jesus' name. Amen.

Posted on Facebook December 3, 2014, 9:45 am

Father God, thank you for this blessed day of victory on the way to destiny that You have made. Thank you for protection throughout the day. Thank you for peace in every activity and interaction this day. Thank you for provision for purpose this day. Bless my family and friends this day. Save, heal, comfort, encourage, strengthen, and deliver. Thank you, Lord! In Jesus' name. Amen. Thank you, Brandi Allen, for sharing.

Text to family Thursday, December 4, 2014 (From Psalm 1)

Blessed are my family members who walk and live not in the counsel of the ungodly, nor stands in the path where sinners walk, nor sits down where the scornful gather. But our delight and desire is in the law of the Lord, and on His law, we habitually meditate by day and by night. And we shall be like a tree firmly planted by the streams of water, ready to bring forth fruit in its season; our leaf also shall not fade or wither, and everything we do shall prosper. Thank you, Lord!

Posted on Facebook Thursday, December 4, 2014, 7:48 am

Father God, thank you for this blessed day of victory that You have made. I rejoice and am glad in it. Blessed are my family members who walk and live not in the counsel of the ungodly, nor stands in the path where sinners walk, nor sits down where the scornful gather. But our delight and desire is in the law of the Lord, and on His law, we habitually meditate by day and by night. And we shall be like a tree firmly planted by the streams of water, ready to bring forth fruit in its season; our leaf also shall not fade or wither; and everything we do shall prosper.

As for me and my house, we shall serve the Lord. Thank you for peace, promotion, provision and protection. Thank you that my family, fitness, finances and future are all blessed. Thank you for satisfying us with long, abundant life and showing us Your salvation. Thank you that no weapon formed against us shall prosper.

Thank you for breakthrough, turnaround, sudden change and supernatural manifestation in my favor. Thank you for wisdom, insight and discernment. Thank you for grace to complete every assignment in excellence.

Bless my family and FB friends. Bless my Pastors and church family. Bless my classmates, colleagues and coworkers. Save, heal, encourage, comfort, strengthen, deliver and provide for every need. Thank you, Lord! In Jesus' mighty and matchless name. Amen.

Posted on Facebook December 7, 2014

Father God, I pray for sweet sleep and wonderful rest for my Pastors and church family. I am still wired from tonight's service even though my eyes are ready to close. Thank you for Your presence in our lives. We've been activated and shifted into our new year. Thanks for supernatural manifestation. In Jesus' name. Amen. Good night for real...

Posted on Facebook December 8, 2014, 6:50 am

Father God, thank you for this new, blessed day of victory that You have made. You are faithful, and I trust You! Thank you for brand new mercies. Thank you for grace for every assignment. Be glorified in and through my life.

Heal our land, Lord. Save souls. Restore broken people and places. Thank you for turnaround and sudden change. Thank you for peace and favor. There is no one like You. There is no one greater than You. Thank you for protection in our going out and coming in. Thank you for protecting our children and schools. Thank you for Your presence in our workplaces and community.

Father, we love You! We adore you and honor You. We bless your holy name. Have Your way this day. In Jesus' name. Amen. Have a great day!

Posted on Facebook Tuesday, December 9, 2014

Father God, thank you for this blessed, new day that You have made. I expect victory. I believe Your report. Thank you, Lord, for showing Yourself strong on my behalf. I trust You. Demonstrate Your power and be glorified in and through my life. Thank you, Lord. In Jesus' mighty and matchless name I pray. Amen. I'm in expectation... have an amazing day! God is able!

Posted on Facebook December 11, 2014

Father God, thank you... today is four months since I have last driven. On July 1st we were hit in a car accident. On July 29th I had a seizure 10 minutes into training at the gym while trying to return to an exercise routine. On August 11th the neurologist said I couldn't drive for 4-6 months. It has been a process...BUT GOD! He is faithful! I have just been medically approved to resume driving. Been praying and believing... now I am prayerful for swift approval from DMV as soon as I get the paperwork turned in. Robert has been a huge support throughout this process... thank you Babe! I love you and appreciate you!

I trust God! Believing for complete healing. Believing to drive again without restrictions. Believing for favor in all matters. Thank you, Lord!

Posted on Facebook December 12, 2014

Father God, thank you for the rain we so desperately need. I pray for no loss of life due to flooding especially in the areas previously damaged by fire. As people travel to work and school, I pray for care and caution. Thank you, Lord. In Jesus' name. Amen.

Posted on Facebook Tuesday, December 16, 2014

Father God, thank you for this blessed day of victory that You have made. I rejoice and am glad in it. Your will be done in and through my life. Your plans for me are for good and not for evil, to give me an expected end. I thank you for satisfying me with long, healthy abundant life and showing me Your salvation. Thank you for showing Yourself strong on my behalf.

Father, bless my family and friends. Comfort those who lost a loved one last night, last week or last year. Heal and restore. Minister to those going through a physical, financial, spiritual, mental or relational challenge. You are faithful and more than able. You can be trusted. Thank you, Lord! In Jesus' mighty name. Amen. Have a dynamic day FB friends! God, is still on the throne. Surrender today...

Posted on Facebook December 17, 2014

Father God, I lift up my 18-year old cousin and all who have made commitments to serve in the armed forces. Be with them and protect them through basic training and beyond. Strengthen them physically, mentally and emotionally. I come against accidents, injury, mistakes, mishaps and premature death. Bless and encourage their family members. Thank you, Lord. In Jesus' name. Amen.

Posted on Facebook Thursday, December 25, 2014, 12:15 am

Merry Christmas to all and to all a good night...Father God, thank you for the gift of Your Son Jesus. Thank you for another year. Thank you for being a very present help.

Comfort those having a hard time due to the loss of a loved one or has a family member/friend who is transitioning at this time.

Heal those with challenges in their body. Encourage those who are discouraged, depressed or tormented in their mind. Minister peace in their midst.

Restore broken relationships. Return the prodigal home. Cover those in abusive relationships. Protect those in need of deliverance and release. Strengthen those who feel hopeless. You are faithful.

Provide for those in need. I lift up those unable to be home with loved ones this holiday season and pray for strength. I pray for those who may have a challenging time in the presence of their loved ones. Heal like only You can.

Thank you, Lord for health, healing and wholeness. Bless my family members, friends, pastors and church family. Jesus is the Reason we celebrate this season.

I pray for those in need of salvation. I pray they would acknowledge the gift of Your Son, recognize their need of forgiveness and receive Your gift Jesus into their heart as Savior and Lord.

I pray for turnaround, sudden change and breakthrough only You can give. Demonstrate your power this day. Heal, deliver and set free this day. Thank you, Lord. In Jesus' name. Amen.

Posted on Facebook Tuesday, December 30, 2014

Father God, thank you for this blessed day of victory. Thank you for your mercy and grace. Thank you for loving us in spite of us. Thank you for protection and peace throughout this day. Thank you for healing and wholeness. Have Your way this day. Thank you, Lord. In Jesus' name. Amen. Be blessed FB friends.

2015

Posted on Facebook Thursday, January 1, 2015

Father God, thank you for this new, blessed day and year of victory. Thank you for Your covering, protection, and provision in 2014. Thank you for the pruning, purging, and correction that took place. I am excited about the plans You have for my family and me in 2015. You are faithful, and I trust in You with all my heart. Thank you that no weapon formed against me or my family shall prosper. Use me for Your glory and demonstrate Your power in and through me. Thank you for my pastors and church family. Order our steps. I pray for breakthrough, turnaround and sudden change in the lives of Your people. Show Yourself strong on our behalf. Lord, thank you! In Jesus' mighty name. Amen.

FB friends, may this be your best year yet! Let's be diligent, disciplined and determined to be and do all God has in store for us to be and do. Happy New Year!

Posted on Facebook January 1, 2015

Father God, I trust You...You are faithful. Minister peace and comfort to those who have lost a loved one. Heal and make whole. Surround them with Your presence. Thank you, Lord! In Jesus' name. Amen. Praying for the Cofield, Deruso and Ayers family.

Posted on Facebook Sunday, January 4, 2015, 7:15 am

Father God, thank you for this new, blessed day of victory that You have made. Thank you for new grace and mercy. Help us to be who You've called us to be.

I pray all needs are met. I pray for salvation for those who have never confessed their sins and believed in/received Your Son Jesus into their heart. I pray for rededication for those who walked away from You due to offense, misunderstanding, discouragement, distractions, relocation or any other life occurrence in general.

I pray for physical, emotional, mental and relational healing and restoration. Heal hearts, hurts, minds and bodies. I pray for supernatural manifestation to take place. I pray for Divine encounters and interactions to take place. I pray for breakthrough, turnaround and sudden change to take place.

I pray for provision, protection, and peace for those in need. I come against demonic interference, activity, and deception keeping Your children in bondage. I come against abuse and addiction. I come against self-sabotage and the spirit of suicide. I come against premature and untimely death. I come against fiery darts/lies of the enemy keeping Your children hostage. I come against confusion, frustration, and irritation.

Father God, demonstrate Your power. Heal, deliver, save, encourage, strengthen, comfort, protect. You are faithful and loving and forgiving. Thank you, Lord, for hearing and answering. In Jesus' mighty name. Amen.

Prayer of salvation and rededication:

Father God, I confess I am a sinner in need of salvation. I believe that Jesus died on the cross for my sins and rose from the dead that I may have eternal life in heaven. By faith, I ask Jesus to come into my heart, forgive me of my sins and be my Savior and Lord. I dedicate and commit to living my life for You. I repent of doing things my way and submit to Your plan for my life. Thank you, Lord. In Jesus' name. Amen.

If you prayed this prayer and believed it in Your heart, this is a new day. Praise God. Ask God for further direction. God Bless You!

Text to WOVEN Cabinet Thursday, January 15, 2015

Father God, thank you for this blessed day of victory that You have made. We declare success over our day and lives. Thank you for Pastor Linda and her vision for WOVEN and her heart for women. We call increase in attendance, finances, maturity, and membership. We declare powerful ministry goes forth whenever we gather. May the cabinet administer the vision with excellence and efficiency. Bless our Pastors, our church, and family. Thank you for a Supernatural year. In Jesus' name. Amen.

Dear Heavenly Father, thank you for this blessed day of victory that You have made. Thank you for health, strength, and wholeness. Thank you for soundness of mind and the movement of my limbs. Thank you for brand new mercies. You are faithful, and I am grateful.

I plead the blood of Jesus over every mode of transportation I will take this day as well as for my colleagues, the HBCU teams, and volunteers traveling across the country for HCASC this weekend. I pray for good weather and safety going and returning. I come against confusion, frustration, and all demonic interference, in Jesus' name.

Father, I lift up my family, church family, and friends and pray for their needs to be met. Heal bodies, minds, hearts and relationships. Encourage, comfort and strengthen all experiencing the loss of a loved one. Saturate with Your presence that brings peace to those who are depressed, discouraged or feel hopeless.

Thank you for another opportunity to give You the praise, honor, and glory due You. There is no one like You. There is no one greater than You. I trust You. Satisfy me with long life and show me Your salvation. Use me for Your glory and demonstrate Your power through me.

Save, heal, comfort, deliver, protect, encourage, provide for, bless all those praying this prayer/reading this post. May they trust in You with all their heart and seek You first. I love You and Thank you, Lord. In Jesus' mighty and matchless name. Amen! Have a fantastic, favor-filled weekend FB friends!

Posted on Facebook January 30, 2015

Father, thank you. I pray for sweet sleep in these next 5 hours. Please send the noisy folks still up to bed. May I be rested and refreshed and ready for a FULL productive day. Thank you, Lord. In Jesus' name. Amen.

Posted on Facebook January 31, 2015

Father God, thank you for this new, blessed day of victory. Go before me to guide and give me wisdom and supernatural strength and insight for a successful, stress-free, productive, peaceful, orderly day. At the end when I need to drive 3 hours back to Baltimore/PA give me clear, safe travel and keep me alert. Thank you for blessing my family and friends. Comfort, heal, strengthen and encourage. In Jesus' name. Amen. UMES HCASC NQT up next...

Posted on Facebook January 31, 2015

Father God, thank you. This has been a long, emotionally intense week, a full weekend of work travel, competition, and long hours on the road. Then my Sunday night flight back to California was canceled due to weather in my connecting city of Chicago. Good night and God bless. Still grateful...

Posted on Facebook Friday, February 6, 2015 (Celebrating the life of a loved one)

Dear Heavenly Father, thank you for this new, blessed day that You have made. I decree and declare victory over this day. Thank you for health, healing, wholeness and soundness of mind. Your compassions fail not. They are new every morning. Thank you for new grace and new mercy. Great is Your faithfulness.

Father, You are not surprised or caught off guard with anything so we can trust You in every situation and circumstance. Your plans for us are for good and not for evil, so we trust You. We submit to the leading of Your Holy Spirit and surrender our plans to You. You promise never to leave us or forsake us, so we trust You.

Father God, I lift up those in need of salvation, healing, provision, peace, deliverance, breakthrough, strength, turnaround, mercy, favor, comfort, sudden change, restoration. You are the only Source of what we need. I pray we trust in You with all our heart leaning not on our own understanding. I pray we seek You, Your Kingdom and Righteousness first. Heal our land.

Father, I lift up my Pastors, church family and everyone connected to Diijon Bishop this day. As we celebrate his life, demonstrate Your power. Be glorified in every prayer, song, spoken word, and an act of love that goes forth. I pray for supernatural manifestation to bring healing, strength, peace, salvation, restoration and reconciliation. I thank you for order. I thank you for Your presence to saturate the sanctuary, and everywhere we gather. I stand still to see Your hand move this day. Cover the children. I plead the blood of Jesus over them and pray that they all walk out the destiny You have for them. I pray they never suffer lack or loss. Be glorified this day.

Lord, comfort and heal all who have suffered the loss of a loved one. Heal grief, regret, and depression. Provide for needs and orchestrate plans to go forth and in order. You are still faithful and can be trusted.

Father, I pray for safe travels going out and coming in and come against accident, injury and all demonic activity. I plead the blood of Jesus over our children and the schools and campuses where they go. Protect them and give them good success in their studies. Bless our families.

Thank you, Lord. In Jesus' mighty and matchless name. Amen.

Posted on Facebook Saturday, February 6, 2015, PM

Father God, before the beginning You knew Diijon would gather family and friends together to celebrate his life and legacy. You knew who would be present and who wouldn't make it to the service today. I lift up everyone connected to him and pray for healing. Touch hearts, minds, and bodies. Calm fears, remove doubts, and heal hurts. I pray for restoration and reconciliation. I pray for total surrender and submission to Your plan for our lives. May we be Holy Spirit led and passionately pursue Your purpose for us. May we walk out our destiny. Bless our pastors and church families. Minister like only You can. Comfort, encourage and strengthen. Thank you for the privilege of knowing Diijon David Bishop. You are faithful. I am grateful, and I trust You. Thank you, Lord! In Jesus' mighty name. Amen.

Posted on Facebook February 11, 2015

Father God, comfort and encourage the Houston and Brown families. I pray for turnaround, healing and complete recovery for Bobbi Kristina. There is nothing impossible for You. Thank you, Lord! In Jesus' mighty name. Amen.

Posted on Facebook February 18, 2015

Father God, I lift up the hurting to You right now. Heal Jehovah Rapha. Thank you, Lord! In Jesus' mighty name. Amen. God is faithful. Trust Him

Posted on Facebook February 19, 2015

Father God, thank you for this blessed day of victory that You have made. I will rejoice and be glad in it. You are my Hope, Source, Strength, Joy, and Peace. I speak peace and productivity over my day. I pray for wisdom, understanding, and discernment to be successful in this day. Thank you for mercy, grace, and forgiveness. Thank you for favor and promotion.

Thank you for never leaving or forsaking me. I lift up my family members and friends to You and pray for physical, mental, emotional, relational, spiritual and financial healing to take place. You are our Provider, Peace, Healer, Comfort, Hope, Deliverer.

I come against confusion, frustration, plans, ploys, and plots from the enemy that would try to hinder, discourage, depress and distract us from fulfilling the destiny You have for us. May we know when an occurrence is an opportunity to grow or an assignment for warfare.

I come against premature, untimely death and pray for protection from accident and injury. Help us to be good stewards over our bodies. I plead the blood of Jesus over everyone and everything connected to me. Satisfy us with long, healthy abundant life and show us Your salvation. Cover everything concerning us. Thank you for a hedge of protection around our schools, homes, workplaces and community. Bless my Pastors and church family.

You are faithful, and I love and trust You. Order my start, steps, and stops. Thank you, Lord. In Jesus' name. Amen.

Posted on Facebook February 19, 2015

Father God, I pray for relief from the extreme weather across the nation especially the snow, ice and now cold. Thank you, Lord! In Jesus' name. Amen.

Posted on Facebook February 28, 2015

Father God, thank you for this blessed day of victory that You have made. Go before us to meet every need. Use us for Your glory. Restore, relax and refresh us. Thank you, Lord. In Jesus' name. Amen.

Posted on Facebook March 11, 2015, 6:14 am

Dear Heavenly Father, thank you for this blessed day of victory that You have made. Thank you for brand new mercies. Great is Your faithfulness. Thank you for sufficient grace for everything we face this day. Thank you for never leaving us or forsaking us. We trust You.

We seek You first. Thank you for Supernatural physical, mental and emotional strength to walk through every situation knowing we are victorious in You. Thank you for health, healing, wholeness and soundness of mind. Thank you for satisfying us with long, abundant life and showing us Your salvation.

Thank you for the relationships, friendships, friends, family members, acquaintances and colleagues in my life. I lift each one up to You and pray for each need. Save, heal, comfort, encourage, strengthen, deliver, protect, provide. You can be trusted. I pray for miracles, signs, and wonders to take place in the lives of those trusting in You as well as those who don't know You.

I pray for breakthrough, turnaround and sudden change where it's needed most. Hear and answer the prayers of the intercessor. We stand on the wall as watchmen over all You have entrusted to us. We will not come down until our assignment is complete.

Thank you for going before us this day to lead, guide and protect from accident, incident or injury and dangers seen and unseen. We are submitted and surrendered to Your plans and purpose for our lives. Show Yourself strong on our behalf this day.

Thank you, thank you, Thank you, Lord. In Jesus' mighty and matchless name. Amen.

Father God, heal heavy and hurting hearts this day. Comfort, encourage and strengthen those experiencing loss. Surround and saturate with Your peace. Provide for the needs and cover and protect. Thank you, Lord! In Jesus' name. Amen.

Posted on Facebook March 18, 2015

Father God, I lift up my Alma Mater Morgan State to You and pray a hedge of protection around the entire campus and plead the blood of Jesus over it and the surrounding community. I pray for peace to reign. I come against demonic activity and influence and the resulting violence when people react instead of responding. Saturate the campus with Your presence. May the focus be on obtaining an education and being successful. Remove anyone and everyone with ill intention. Heal those hurt in the altercations. I pray for wisdom for the administration, faculty, and staff. I pray for godly decision-making in the affairs of the university. Prosper Morgan so that it continues to produce leaders and scholars with character and integrity. I come against confusion particularly heightened from media coverage of the negative. I speak life over Morgan State. Thank you, Lord. In Jesus' name. Amen.

Posted on Facebook March 21, 2015

Father God, thank you for this new and blessed day that You have made. I pray for safe travels for everyone headed to HCASC today. I pray for supernatural strength for me and everyone running on little to no sleep. I speak peace, order, and productivity over this day. I lift up my family, friends and loved ones and pray for their needs... heal, comfort, encourage and strengthen. Protect and provide this day. Thank you, Lord. You are faithful! In Jesus' name, I pray. Amen. Have a great day!

Posted on Facebook March 22, 2015

Father God, You are Jehovah Rapha, and I know You to be my Healer. I pray for supernatural strength in my body and a soothing touch in my throat so I can speak without discomfort and communicate clearly for the next 15 hours. Thank you, Lord, for this new day that You have made. Thank you for my family and friends. Bless each one. In Jesus' name. Amen.

Posted on Facebook April 1, 2015

Father God, thank you for this new, blessed day that You have made. I thank you for this new month and the victory that's ahead. My fitness, family members, finances are all blessed, and my future is bright. You are in control, and I trust You. I am grateful and glad. Thank you for all You have connected to me. Move in their lives for their good and Your glory. Use me to bless others. Thank you, Lord! In Jesus' name. Amen.

Posted on Facebook April 5, 2015

Father God, thank you for Your sacrifice that provided salvation and eternal security. I lift up every service that will take place tomorrow and pray that the pews and chairs are filled, as well as the altars. I pray for salvation decisions and rededications. I pray for healing to manifest. I pray for repentance and restoration. I pray for lives to be changed.

I come against distractions and demonic interference that would try to hinder real change. I pray for peace in every home. I pray for provision for every need. I pray Your people will be ready to receive the harvest of souls. Demonstrate Your power. Thank you, Lord. In Jesus' mighty name. Amen.

Posted on Facebook April 15, 2015

Father God, thank you for this blessed day of victory that You have made. We are another day closer to fulfilling purpose and destiny by walking in total submission to Your will. Order my steps God. You are faithful. Thank you, Lord. In Jesus' name. Amen. Have an amazing day FB friends.

Posted on Facebook April 16, 2015

Father God, thank you for blessing my dad with another year of life today and satisfying both of my parents with long, healthy, abundant life and showing them Your salvation. In Jesus' name, amen.

Text to Hubby April 16, 2015

Father God, thank you for this new day. Thank you for covering Robert from the crown of his head to the soles of his feet. Thank you for victory in every step he takes. Your Son overcame so he can overcome situations and circumstances. I come against fear, worry, and anxiety and speak peace and prosperity over Robert. Thank you for break-through, turnaround and answered prayer. In Jesus' name. Amen. Love you, Babe

Posted on Facebook April 19, 2015

It's time again... assignments and projects to complete and no distractions allowed, so I'll be staying away from social media for a few.

Father God, You are faithful. Thank you for the plans You have for me. Help me to be diligent and disciplined in every area. Thank you for health and wholeness in every area.

Thank you that my family, finances, fitness and future are all blessed. Minister to the needs of my Facebook friends. Heal, comfort, save, strengthen, encourage, deliver, protect, promote and provide resources. Thank you, Lord, for open doors. Thank you for new mercy every day. Thank you for forgiveness and favor. Thank you for salvation and eternal security.

There is no one like You. There is no one greater than You. I believe and expect supernatural manifestation in my life and the lives of my loved ones. Use me for Your glory. Thank you, Lord. In Jesus' name. Amen.

Text to Hubby April 20, 2015

Father God, we trust You with our future. I pray for wisdom and discernment in how, when and where to move. Keep us encouraged in the meantime. May we please You with our lives. You are faithful.

Saturate Anthem and College Bowl Holy Spirit. Thank you, Lord. In Jesus' name. Amen. Love you!

Posted on Facebook April 27, 2015

Father God, I lift up the city of Baltimore to You at this time and pray for peace and calm to saturate the community. I come against confusion, frustration, distraction and demonic influence over the minds of those acting out of anger. I pray for protection and plead the blood of Jesus over law enforcement officers and other first responders as well as over businesses, churches, schools and homes. I pray for wisdom for the decision-makers. I come against premature/untimely death. I pray for the Church of the Living God to unite, take authority and use their faith for change. You said in Your Word if we would humble ourselves, pray, seek Your face and turn from our wicked ways then You would hear from heaven, forgive our sins and heal our land. I pray this for every city in our nation. Heal our land, God. Thank you, Lord. In Jesus' name. Amen.

Posted on Facebook April 27, 2015

Dear Heavenly Father, I lift up all in need of a change in position, situation or circumstances right now whether physically, mentally, emotionally, relationally, financially or spiritually.

Heal every wound. Meet every need. Restore joy and hope in You. I come against discouragement, depression and demonic encroachments that come to hinder destiny. I pray for healing, comfort, encouragement, deliverance and peace.

Father, I pray for the rescue and recovery situation in Nepal. I lift up family members left behind. Provide for their needs. I pray for recovery in Baltimore. I arrest every spirit driving souls to cause destruction. I pray for salvation and repentance. It's not too late for real change to take place. Reveal and remove anyone with ill intent from positions of authority. I pray for restored order. I pray for answers and resources to the problems and workers to carry out the plan. Thank you, Lord, for hearing and answering. In Jesus' name. Amen.

Posted on Facebook May 7, 2015

Father God, I thank you for this blessed day of victory that You have made. I pray for America to return to You and truly trust in You. I pray for protection over our borders, communities, and homes. I pray for healing to take place in our land. I pray for Your people to humble themselves, pray, seek Your face and turn from our wicked ways not just today but every day. You are faithful to watch over Your Word to perform it. Thank you for going before me to make crooked places straight and grant me favor. I love You and trust You, Lord. Thank you, Father. I declare my family, fitness, finances and future are already blessed. In Jesus' mighty name. Amen.

Posted on Facebook May 11, 2015

Father God, thank you for this new, blessed day of victory. Thank you for health, healing, wholeness and soundness of mind. Thank you for another day to say thank you. You are worthy to be praised!

Thank you for going before us this day and week to make the crooked places straight. Thank for protection in our going out and coming in. Thank you for provision and favor for every need and assignment.

We declare peace, order, and productivity over our day and week. Equip us to carry out Your plan for our lives. Thank you for promotion and elevation. We are submitted and surrendered to You and trust You. We thank you for supernatural manifestation this day, week and month. We are not moved by what we see, hear or feel. We are focused and fixed in faith on You. Use us for Your glory. Demonstrate Your power in and through Your people. Show Yourself strong on our behalf.

I lift up my family members, Facebook friends, and everyone connected to me and pray for needs to be met. Save, heal, comfort, encourage, deliver, provide for and protect. Restore broken relationships.

Bless my pastors and church family this day and week. Thank you for this Kingdom connection. LPCC is a lighthouse in our communities. We walk in love and unity with one another fulfilling vision. Thank you for increase and overflow to complete purpose. Thank you, Lord, for hearing and answering. In Jesus' mighty name. Amen.

Posted on Facebook May 14, 2015

Father God, thank you for this blessed day of victory. Thank you for protection as we slept. Thank you for another opportunity to serve You. Help me to be who You've called me to be.

I lift up the hurting to You right now. Comfort those who have experienced sudden, tragic loss as well as those who have cared for a loved one who has passed on through the night or may be currently transitioning. Strengthen those overcoming a challenging diagnosis and remind them that You are Jehovah Rapha, their Healer. Encourage those who have been knocked down from life's situations and circumstances and feel hopeless, depressed or discouraged. You are their Source of strength and hope. You are their Way up and out.

Father, thank you for mercy, grace, and forgiveness. Thank you for turnaround, reversal and sudden change. Thank you for favor, increase and overflow. Thank you for healing, wholeness, and restoration. You are faithful and can be trusted. Demonstrate Your power. Bless me to be a blessing and use me for Your glory. Thank you for my family of faith. Order my steps and orchestrate my assignments. I thank You and love You, Lord. In Jesus' mighty name. Amen.

Posted on Facebook May 15, 2015

Father God, thank you for this blessed day of victory and success. Thank you for a mistake-free dental surgery without complications. Thank you for accuracy before, during and after the procedure. Thank you, Jehovah Rapha for quick and complete healing without infection. Thank you for supernatural manifestation throughout this process. Thank you for provision. Thank you for peace of mind. Thank you for the appropriate level of pain medicine without negative side effects. Be glorified this day. Heal, comfort, save, strengthen, encourage, deliver, protect, provide for those in need. Demonstrate Your power this day. Thank you, Lord! In Jesus' name. Amen.

Here are snippets of my Friday night in Orange County. Father God, thank you for divine appointments, assignments, and encounters. Thank you for the fellowship and conversation with my sister and friend. Thank you for the change and transformation that is already taking place in our lives, homes, and families for our good and Your glory. Thank you for fresh vision and provision for what You've called me/us to do. Thank you for refreshing and restoring me and preparing me for what's next. You love me, and I am grateful. Thank you for loving me so. In Jesus' name. Amen.

Posted on Facebook May 23, 2015

Father, thank you for this long day of fellowship, ministry, outreach and fun family time. Thank you for safe travels from Dana Point at 6:45 am to AV by 10 a.m. via a stop in the SFV and then back home tonight by 10:30 pm from Carson after picking up family from LAX arriving for a summer internship (a pleasant surprise for the girls). I am blessed. We are blessed. I love productivity and thank you for growing me. Rest us tonight so that we may all wake refreshed in the morning. Bless all who sowed time, talent and treasure to make a difference in the lives of others in need. Move in a mighty way in the lives of all who received ministry this day. Thank you, Lord. You are faithful. In Jesus' name. Amen.

Posted on Facebook May 25, 2015

Birthday Blessings to 2 amazing, anointed, powerful preachers. Your assignment to the nations is great, and God has gifted you and prepared you for such a time as this. I am grateful for you.

Father God, I lift up Dr. Antoinette Hewitt and Pastor Lola Carter Hester to You and pray Your blessings overtake them today and beyond. Use them for Your glory and continue to demonstrate Your power in and through their lives. I pray for open doors of opportunity, promotion, and elevation. Enlarge their territory and increase their influence. You know who needs to hear what You've placed in their mouth. Thank you for provision for the vision. Thank you for their submission to Your call.

Satisfy them with long, abundant life and show them Your salvation. Thank you, Lord! In Jesus' name. Amen.

Happy, Happy Birthday! Enjoy! ☺

Posted on Facebook May 28, 2015

Father, thank you for healing, for helping, for saving, for providing, for comforting, for strengthening, for delivering, for restoring, for transforming, for promoting, for protecting, for encouraging, for forgiving, for being God.

Posted on Facebook June 6, 2015

Father God, I lift up my Pastors and church family of Living Praise Christian Center to You and pray Your perfect will be done in and through our lives. We submit our will to Yours. We are in expectation of supernatural manifestation in our congregation. We are in anticipation of miracles, signs, and wonders. We gather in person or via Cyber Church with excitement ready to engage You in intense worship. It's a new day and a new season. We are ready to receive the harvest and fulfill the assignment You have called us to do. We believe souls will be saved, hearts will be encouraged, lives will be changed, relationships will be restored, and bodies will be healed whenever we gather. Holy Spirit, have Your way. Thank you for Dr. Fred and Pastor Linda Hodge. Continue to use them for Your glory and bless them to be a blessing. In Jesus' mighty and matchless name. Amen.

Posted on Facebook June 9, 2015

Glory to God! Hallelujah! Father God, thank you for supernatural manifestation. Thank you for miracles, signs, and wonders. As I sit waiting for the neurologist for my follow-up, this is a timely faith builder for believing for healing in my body. I've been healed and free of seizures before (over 30+ years ago) and will walk free of seizures without medication again. You are Faithful. You are my Healer. Demonstrate Your power, Lord. In Jesus' name. Amen.

Posted on Facebook June 27, 2015, 7:35 am

Dear Heavenly Father, thank you for this new day. I am not moved by what I see, hear or feel because You are still seated on the throne. You are faithful, and I trust You. You are worthy of all our praise, glory and honor. I pray for salvation, healing, and deliverance for every family member. I pray for repentance and restoration. I come against generational curses, demonic activity, and self-sabotage. Satan cannot destroy what he did not create. I pray for breakthrough, turnaround and sudden change. I pray for mercy, grace, and forgiveness. I pray we submit and surrender our plans to Your plans. Cover and protect every family member. I plead the blood of Jesus over everyone. Thank you, Lord, for the victory. In Jesus' name. Amen. Trust and Serve God. He loves YOU!

Posted on Facebook July 1, 2015

Father God, thank you for this blessed day of victory that You have made. Thank you for new grace and mercy. Thank you for seeing us through the first half of 2015. Nothing caught You by surprise so we can continue to trust You and walk by faith and not in fear. What You didn't order, You allowed. You are faithful and more than able.

As we look towards 12/31/15, I pray we draw closer to You and stronger in You in this season. I pray for grace for every situation and circumstance. I pray to be fixed and focused in the center of Your perfect will for my life. Order my steps. Holy Spirit, be my Guide.

Lord, I lift up to You those in need... of salvation, of healing, of wholeness, of deliverance, of restoration, of provision, of protection, of comfort, of peace, of strength, of encouragement, of the miraculous, of hope, of covering, of guidance, of shelter, of rest, of love. You are all we need. You hold the key to true happiness. You are our Source.

I pray for physical, mental, emotional, and relational healing. I pray for accurate diagnosis and treatment. I pray for supernatural signs and wonders.

I pray for open doors of employment, promotion, business and opportunity. I pray for finances to increase and for provision for our God-given vision. Thank you for favor.

I pray for spiritual healing, for forgiveness and repentance. I pray for Your people to humble ourselves, pray, seek Your face and turn from our wicked ways. I pray we walk in the Word and not after the flesh. I pray for renewal and revival to take place. I pray for honesty and integrity to govern our lives.

Father, I am in expectation of miracles, signs, and wonders. I am in expectation for prayers to be answered. Move in the lives of my family members, neighbors, pastors, church family, classmates, coworkers, colleagues calling on You. Hear the prayer of the intercessor. You have given us free will. May we choose wisely.

Reveal and remove anything or anyone not ordained by You. I come against demonic activity and interference. I come against distractions that would delay destiny being fulfilled. I come against premature, untimely death. I pray for wisdom, insight, and discernment. I pray for discipline and diligence to do what You've called us to do. I pray for divine assignments and encounters and mutually-beneficial relationships. Thank you for breakthrough, turnaround and sudden change. Thank you for favor. Thank you for satisfying us with long life and showing us Your salvation.

I give You all the praise, glory and honor. There is no one like You. There is no one greater than You. Demonstrate Your power on my behalf. Thank you, Lord. In Jesus' mighty and matchless name. Amen. Have an amazing month!

Posted on Facebook July 9, 2015

Father God, thank you for this new, blessed day of victory that You have made. I shall rejoice and be glad in it. Thank you for the women You have called to the 2015 Daughters of Divine Destiny conference this weekend. I lift up Dr. Micheline, Pastor Linda and every ministry gift to You. Use them mightily for Your glory. Cover and strengthen them. I pray for protection and safe travels for everyone going and coming. I pray for rich impartation that results in revival and real change. Demonstrate Your power. Thank you for divine appointments, assignments, and encounters. Thank you for destiny and purpose being realized and fulfilled. I come against delays, distractions, and detours not appointed by You. I give You all the glory, honor and praise. In Jesus' mighty name. Amen.

Posted on Facebook July 10, 2015

Father God, we lift up Pastor Linda to You and pray You use her in a mighty way as she ministers to the Called and Chosen women this morning. Thank you that the resources we brought are bought to continue to minister to the women and the churches they represent. Let us sell out everything that is not given away. Demonstrate Your power this day. Thank you, Lord. In Jesus' name. Amen.

Posted on Facebook July 11, 2015

Father God, thank you for this wonderful time of refreshing and impartation in the desert. Continue to pour into the ministry gifts so that they may pour out on us. I lift up our conference host Dr. Micheline McFarland, my mentor Pastor Linda Hodge, Teacher Joyce Esteves, and Prophetess Saundra O'Neal. Rest us all as we sleep tonight. Exceed our expectations in the morning session. Demonstrate Your power. Bless every attendee, participant, committee member and support team. Thank you, Lord, for this new season. Thank you for the shift that has already taken place in our homes and churches. In Jesus' mighty name. Amen.

Posted on Facebook July 19, 2015

Father God, this is the day that You have made. I will rejoice and be glad in it. In You we have victory. In You we have peace. In You we have hope. In You we have healing. In You we have strength. In You we have joy. In You we have protection and provision. In You we have forgiveness, mercy, and grace. In You is all we need.

Father, I lift up all those in need right now. I pray they would seek You and surrender to You. You are able and faithful, no matter what. Save, heal, comfort, encourage, deliver, set free, strengthen, restore, protect, provide.

Nothing that happens catches You by surprise, so we trust You. You are sovereign. You are loving. You are caring. You are waiting for us to come and call on You. Great is Your faithfulness.

Minister to my family members, friends, associates, neighbors, and acquaintances. Demonstrate Your power. I believe for supernatural manifestation. Thank you, Lord! In Jesus' mighty name. Amen.

Posted on Facebook July 23, 2015

Father God, thank you for this blessed day of victory that You have made. I rejoice and am glad. You make no mistakes, so I read tomorrow's devotion today on purpose.

Therefore, I lift up everyone who has been or continue to be bullied. I pray for mental and emotional healing. I pray for physical and financial restoration. Send help and support to those in need. Cover and protect in every arena where it's taking place.

I lift up the bully and pray for conviction. Make the bully uncomfortable and heal the hurt and whatever is causing that behavior.

Father God, I come against bullying from the playground to the boardroom. I pray for healthy relationships and interactions in our schools, on our university/college campuses and in our communities and courtrooms. Surround and saturate with Your presence.

I pray for turnaround and resolution in any domestic violence situation which is also bullying. Heal Lord. Help Lord this day.

Strengthen, encourage and provide a way of escape. God, You are faithful. You understand because You too were bullied. Thank you for the shed blood and broken body of Your Son Jesus for us. Through Him, we can have salvation and eternal security. Heal Lord today. In Jesus' mighty name. Amen.

Posted on Facebook July 27, 2015

Father God, thank for another day that You have made. Thank you for victory and favor in this day. Thank you for peace and productivity in this day. Thank you for healing and wholeness this day. Thank you for reversal and restoration this day. Thank you for new mercy and grace this day. Thank you for forgiveness and protection this day. I love You, Lord, and I am grateful. Thank you for never leaving or forsaking me. Thank you for Your good plans for me.

Dear Heavenly Father, save, heal, deliver, comfort, encourage, protect, strengthen and provide for those in need and calling on You now. Send help to those in need but don't know they are in need. Minister to those who feel stuck, discouraged, depressed, hopeless. Surround them with peace only You can give. You are the Way, the Truth, and the Life. You are faithful, loving, caring and able. Expose the plans of the enemy and provide the solution to the situation. Send laborers in to Your harvest.

Thank you, Lord. There is no one like You. There is no one greater than You. I trust You. I will forever serve You. Demonstrate Your power this day. Thank you, Lord. In Jesus' name. Amen. Happy Blessed Monday! Have a great week. Finish July strong!

Posted on Facebook July 29, 2015

Father God, You continue to be faithful in my life. Thank you for keeping me from a year ago from today when I had a seizure. I believe for complete healing without medication. Great is Your faithfulness, and I trust You. You continue to guide, protect and provide. Thank you, Lord. In Jesus' name. Amen.

Posted on Facebook July 31, 2015

Father God, thank you for never leaving me or forsaking me. Thank you for always protecting me and providing for me. Thank you for always guiding and directing me. Thank you for being my strength and support. Thank you for prompting me to step out of the boat yet again. Your plans are to prosper me. They are plans for good and not evil, and I trust You with my life.

As I step into a new season, show Yourself strong on my behalf. Use me for Your glory to make a difference for Your Kingdom and in my community. Thank you for favor and open doors of opportunity. Thank you for provision for the vision and mutually beneficial relationships. Order my steps and orchestrate my plans. I am excited and in expectation for Supernatural manifestation to take place in my life and the lives of those connected to me.

Thank you for salvation, healing, and wholeness. Thank you for victory in every area. I see me as You see me. Thank you, Lord, for my new day. In Jesus' name. Amen.

Posted on Facebook August 10, 2015

This is the day that the Lord has made. Let us rejoice and be glad in it. Father God, I thank you for this blessed day and week of victory. I declare peace and productivity over this day and week. I thank you for good success over this day and week. Thank you for protection as we go out and come in. Thank you for provision for the vision and direction to carry out destiny.

Father, as our children return to school and college, we plead the blood of Jesus over them. Surround them and keep a hedge of protection around their minds. We come against distractions, deception and demonic activities that would try to hinder or delay their success and progress or detour them from fulfilling Your plans and purpose for their lives.

Father, I lift up everyone going through a physical, mental, emotional, spiritual, relational or financial challenge right now. Heal, deliver, save, restore, provide. You are faithful. I pray for accurate diagnosis and treatment. I pray for complete healing and recovery. I come against complications and infections. I come against premature, untimely death. I come against depression, discouragement, oppression and the spirit of suicide. I pray for miracles, signs, and wonders even now. I pray for breakthrough, turnaround and sudden change. I pray for favor and finances.

Father, I lift up the caregiver and intercessor and pray for physical, mental, and emotional strength. I pray for tenacity and determination to stand. I pray for clarity of mind and wisdom to fulfill the assignment. Send help where it is needed. Thank you for sending laborers into Your harvest.

Thank you, Lord, for victory. Thank you, Lord, for favor. Thank you, Lord, for resources. Thank you, Lord, for mutually beneficial relationships and partnerships. Thank you, Lord, for salvation for our unsaved family members and loved ones. Thank you, Lord, for deliverance for those in darkness and confusion. Thank you for restoration for those who have left or separated from their set place.

Father God, may we walk in righteousness and holiness and obedience to Your Word. May we walk in love and humility as we submit to You. Thank you for satisfying us with long, healthy, abundant life and showing us Your salvation. Thank you for covering us from backlash as we go forth in purpose this day. You are faithful, and we trust You. Use us for Your glory. Demonstrate Your power in and through our lives. We give you praise, honor, and glory. In Jesus' mighty name. Amen.

Posted on Facebook August 12, 2015

Father God, as we prepare for the start of school with orientations today and tomorrow, I pray for eager and excited students and cooperative and supportive parents. I pray for double the number of PTSA membership over last year and active and involved school community. I pray for great communication among the administration, staff, faculty, students and families. I pray for good success and safety this year. Use me for your glory. Thank you, Lord. In Jesus' name. Amen.

Posted on Facebook August 15, 2015

Father God, I lift up our children, family members and friends, whether young or older, to You and pray for healing and deliverance from drug and alcohol abuse and addiction. I pray for protection from abuse of every kind, peer pressure and bullying even from family members and those who are supposed to love and cover their victim. Rescue right now.

I pray for healing from low self-esteem, depression, and discouragement. Minister peace and emotional and mental strength. Heal the hurt. Deliver the broken and those crying out for change. Shine Your light in their dark place.

Father, I pray for breakthrough, turnaround and sudden change in that situation that seems hopeless. I pray for conviction for the one who is negatively impacting the life of another. Heal their hurt as hurting people hurt others.

All things are possible with You God. Provide hope and a way of escape. Set free today. Save today. Heal today. Comfort today. Encourage today. Do it today. God, You are faithful. Thank you, Lord, for hearing and answering. In Jesus' mighty name. Amen.

God loves YOU. Jesus died for YOU. Accept Jesus today through His Father God and experience change only He can bring. I'm praying for YOU.

Posted on Facebook August 17, 2015

Thank you, Father, for this blessed day of victory that You have made. Thank you for favor and good success. Thank you for protection and provision. Thank you for healing and wholeness. Thank you for salvation and security. Thank you, Holy Spirit for wisdom and direction. I love You Lord and thank You. Thank you for supernatural manifestation, miracles, signs, and wonders. Thank you for breakthrough and turnaround. In Jesus' name. Amen.

Posted on Facebook August 18, 2015

Father God, thank you for this new, blessed day of victory that You have made. I rejoice, and I am glad. Thank you for the start of another school year as LAUSD students return today. I pray for safe travels going and coming. I pray for good success in the classroom and safety on the campus. I pray the administrators, faculty and staff and parents would have a renewed commitment to education and instruction. I pray for cooperation between the families and schools. I pray for peace and productivity. Even on this first day if a teacher or other employee needs to be removed, reveal it. I pray for a healthy learning environment in school and at home. Minister to every need. I pray for wisdom and direction both as a parent and PTSA president. Thank you, Lord. In Jesus' name. Amen.

Text to Rose Family August 19, 2015

Father God, thank you for this new, blessed day that You have made. I pray for a hedge of protection around Jennifer and Maya. I pray they hunger and thirst after righteousness. I pray they walk in holiness submitted to You. I pray they trust in You with all their heart. I pray they seek You first. I come against disobedience, disrespect, and distractions and pray for discipline and diligence in all they must do. I plead the blood of Jesus over them and bind their mind to the mind of Christ. Cover them and guide their decision making. I declare peace and productivity over their lives. Thank you, Lord. In Jesus' name. Amen. Love you...

Father God, thank you for this blessed day of victory that You have made. I rejoice and am glad in it. Thank you for the rain watering the earth. Thank you for protection in our going out and coming in. Thank you for favor and productivity. Thank you for peace over our day and week. Thank you for good success.

Father, You are faithful, and I trust You. Thank you for wisdom, direction, and discernment. Thank you for increase, overflow, and Supernatural manifestation. Thank you for healing and breakthrough. Thank you for wholeness and soundness of mind. Thank you for new grace and mercy. Thank you for miracles, signs, and wonders this day. Thank you for turnaround and sudden change. Thank you for satisfying us with long, abundant life and showing us Your salvation. I plead the blood of Jesus over our schools, universities, and communities. Heal our land, Lord.

Father God, I pray for those in need. Heal, save, deliver, protect, provide for, restore, rescue and intervene. Shine Your light into the dark places. I come against discouragement, despair, depression and deception of the enemy. Saturate the confused and frustrated with Your peace. Surround everyone calling on You and cover those being prayed for right now. Demonstrate Your power, Lord. Show Yourself strong on behalf of Your people. There is no one greater than You. There is nothing impossible for You. We trust You. Thank you, Lord. In Jesus' name. Amen.

Father God, I am grateful for this blessed day of victory that You have made. Thank you for grace for this day and all that is in store. You are faithful, and I trust You. I declare peace over this day. My steps are ordered by You.

Cover this day from start to finish. Orchestrate and arrange activities and events. Manage all movement. Restore, refresh, heal and make whole. Demonstrate Your power in the lives of Your people. You are faithful, and I trust You.

Thank you for protection throughout the day. I lift up everyone connected to me and pray for needs to be met. I pray for salvation decisions this day. I pray for Supernatural manifestation this day. Deliver and set free. Thank you, Lord. In Jesus' name. Amen.

Posted on Facebook September 24, 2015

Father God, thank you for this new and blessed day of victory that You have made. I choose to rejoice and be glad in it. Thank you for new mercy and new grace. Great is Your faithfulness.

Thank you for waking and raising me up this morning. Thank you for breath in my body. Thank you for health, strength, and soundness of mind. Thank you for another chance to say thank you. Thank you for never leaving or forsaking me.

Thank you for peace, prosperity, protection and productivity. Thank you for Your plans for me are good and not for evil. Thank you for favor, increase and overflow. Thank you for turnaround and breakthrough. Thank you for supernatural manifestation.

Thank you for restoration of and forgiveness in God-ordained, mutually beneficial relationships. Thank you for salvation and deliverance for my family members, friends, and loved ones. Thank you for miracles, signs, and wonders in the lives of Your people. Thank you for purpose and destiny fulfilled. Thank you for this new day.

Thank you for blessing me to be a blessing. Thank you for divine assignments and encounters. Thank you for ordering my steps and orchestrating my life. Thank you for promotion and elevation. Thank you for acceleration and grace for every situation. Thank you for direction and discernment. Thank you for discipline and diligence. Thank you for calling me and equipping me. I trust You.

Thank you for satisfying me with long life and showing me Your salvation. Thank you for showing Yourself strong on my behalf. Thank you for demonstrating Your power in my life. Thank you for hearing from heaven, forgiving our sins and healing our land. Thank you for this new day! In Jesus' mighty name. Amen. Glory! Hallelujah!

Posted on Facebook September 30, 2015

Father God, thank you for this blessed day of victory that You have made. I rejoice and am glad in it. Thank you for change, transformation and transition that brings me closer to fulfilling purpose and destiny. Thank you for Your plans for me. I declare my family is blessed, my fitness is blessed, my finances are blessed, and my future is blessed and bright. I see success and visualize victory.

I shall finish 2015 strong and give it my all. I can do all things through Christ who strengthens me. This last quarter will be the best of 2015. I am in expectation and anticipation for God's favor on my life to manifest in supernatural ways. I trust You, God. Use me for Your glory and bless me to be a blessing. As for me and my house, we shall serve the Lord continually. I declare peace, protection, promotion and prosperity over my life. No weapon formed against my family or me shall prosper. You are faithful. Thank you for grace, wisdom, and understanding for every assignment. Thank you for discernment in every situation. I walk in discipline and diligence and whatever I put my hands to do prospers. Thank you, Father! Thank you, Jesus! Thank you, Holy Spirit! I give You all praise, glory, and honor. In the mighty and matchless name of Jesus I pray, amen.

Posted on Facebook October 12, 2015

Father God, thank you for this new and blessed day of victory that You have made. I rejoice. I'm grateful and I'm glad. Thank you for the wonderful opportunity to celebrate my mom's 70 years of living. You are so faithful. Keep her in great health, strength, and soundness of mind. Thank you, Lord. In Jesus' name. Amen.

Posted on Facebook October 21, 2015, 10:08 am

Dear Heavenly Father, thank you. This is the day that You have made. I am grateful, glad, and I rejoice in it. I thank you for this momentary detour. Thank you for the opportunity to pause and reflect and be refreshed. Thank you for Your continued faithfulness no matter what the current situation or circumstance may be. You cause all things to work together for our good and Your glory. You can be trusted, and I know victory is mine. Your Joy is my strength, and Your Strength is my joy. Thank you for always being right on time. Thank you for peace that passes all understanding. Thank you for provision for every need. Thank you for protection from dangers seen and unseen. Thank you for Your constant presence.

Lord, I lift up everyone in need. Heal, deliver, save, encourage, comfort, rescue, set free, restore, provide for, strengthen. I pray for Supernatural manifestation in the classroom, courtroom, operating room or wherever Your presence is needed. I pray for miracles, signs, and wonders. Demonstrate Your power. Minister to Your people and move on behalf of those we are interceding for. I believe for breakthrough, turnaround and sudden change. I am in expectation of the impossible. Show Yourself strong on my behalf. Thank you, Lord, for health, strength, and soundness of mind for me and my family members and my loved ones. Thank you, Lord, for satisfying us with long, abundant life and showing us Your salvation. I give You all praise, honor, and glory. Order my steps and direct my path. In the mighty and matchless name of Jesus, I pray. Amen.

Posted on Facebook October 31, 2015

Father God, thank you for Your continued faithfulness in our lives. I lift up to You those depressed, discouraged or in despair right now. I pray for hope and the will to live. The enemy comes to steal, kill and destroy but You have come to give life and that more abundantly. Surround him or her with Your presence. May they call on You from whatever situation, circumstance or position they are experiencing. There is power in the Name of Jesus.

Father, I lift up those with diagnosed or undiagnosed mental challenges. I pray for healing and soundness of mind. I pray for reversal in the mind and body. I pray for relationships to be mended. I pray for strength both physical and emotional for the caregivers and family members. Demonstrate Your power.

Father God, heal, save, encourage, deliver, protect, comfort, cover and provide for those in need. You see all and know all. I believe

You for turnaround and transformation. I believe You for change and breakthrough.

I pray for preservation of life. I pray for supernatural manifestation. I plead the blood of Jesus over our homes, schools, churches and communities and come against death and destruction. Thank you for this new day as it is just past midnight. Shine Your light in every dark place. Bring Your peace to every hostile atmosphere.

To you who are wanting to end it all, GOD LOVES YOU. You have purpose. You have a reason to live. Trust Jesus! Call on Jesus. Call 9-1-1 for help in the natural. I believe in YOU.

Thank you, Lord, for the victory. I give You praise, honor, and glory. In Jesus' mighty name. Amen.

Posted on Facebook November 5, 2015

Father God, thank you for this new and blessed day of victory that You have made. I pray for protection for every family member and FB friend traveling today by land, air, rail or sea. I declare peace over this day and speak peace to the earth and air. Tectonic plates, be still. Save, heal, comfort, encourage, deliver, provide for those in need right now. Surround our schools and communities with Your presence. Order and orchestrate my day, weekend, and month. You are faithful. Thank you, Lord. In Jesus' name. Amen.

Text to Hubby November 8, 2015

Father God, thank you for this blessed day that You have made. Minister to and strengthen Robert for this day. Keep him encouraged and peaceful. May the dinner be a good time of family fellowship. Thank you, Lord! In Jesus' name. Amen.

Posted on Facebook November 13, 2015

Father God, thank you for this blessed day of victory that You have made. I will rejoice and be glad. Thank you for new mercy and new grace. Thank you for healing, wholeness, and soundness of mind. Thank you for supernatural manifestation. Great is Your faithfulness!

I plead the blood of Jesus over this day and my family and everyone connected to me. Protect us in our going out and our coming in. I pray a hedge of protection around and over everywhere our feet should step this day and month. Thank you for giving Your angels charge over us.

Father God, comfort those who have suffered loss. Heal those who are sick and have gone through surgery. Strengthen and encourage those awaiting a procedure. Save those who are loss or feel hopeless. Deliver those in a difficult place. Provide for those in need. You are faithful!

Demonstrate Your power this day. I lift up every Veteran and their family. I pray for physical, mental and emotional healing. I pray for others who have been impacted by trauma, injury or loss. Provide the needed resources whether physical, financial or relational.

I speak peace over this day. I thank you for favor this day. I receive forgiveness this day. I choose joy this day. I claim victory this day. I thank you for healing this day. Use me to be a blessing this day. I expect breakthrough, turnaround and sudden change this day.

I lift up the person reading this prayer and pray for a personal, life-changing encounter with You before we leave 2015. I pray for a shift in their life only You can bring about. Restore and deliver. Save and set free. Promote and elevate. Demonstrate Your power in the lives of Your people. I am excited and in expectation. Thank you, Lord. In Jesus' name. Amen.

Posted on Facebook December 15, 2015

Father God, thank you for this blessed day of victory that You have made. I rejoice and am glad in it. I lift up the LAUSD system and plead the blood of Jesus over every school, administrative office and staff. I pray for wisdom in handling the "credible terror threat" received. I pray for protection for the children already traveling to school who will be sent home. I pray for safety and childcare arrangements where parents and guardians must report to work. Minister to the principals and school personnel that must report today. Father, reveal the source and plan of this threat this day and let everything return to normal tomorrow. I thank you that no weapon formed against our families, our children shall prosper. Thank you, Lord. In Jesus' name. Amen.

193

Posted on Facebook December 16, 2015

Father God, thank you for another blessed day of victory that You have made. Thank you for another chance to say thank you. Thank you for fresh grace and new mercy. Thank you for forgiveness. Thank you for favor.

I speak peace over this day. I pray for unity and order and come against frustration and confusion. I plead the blood of Jesus over all of our schools especially LAUSD this day. I come against negative commentary that would tear down and not build up. I pray for comfort for the family members, friends and classmates of the young man killed on his way to school yesterday. I pray for the driver of the city truck who killed him. Heal Lord!

Father, demonstrate Your power. I pray for focus on success and finishing this school semester of 2015 strong. I pray for wise counsel. I pray for protection and productivity. Orchestrate schedules as events are rearranged. Minister to families and meet needs during this adjustment.

You are faithful. Thank you, Lord. In Jesus' mighty name. Amen.

Posted on Facebook December 22, 2015

Father God, thank you for this new, blessed day of victory that You have made. I declare peace over this day. Thank you for favor, productivity and protection. You are faithful. I trust You. Cover and surround my family members and friends and show Yourself strong on their behalf. Thank you, Lord. In Jesus' name. Amen!

Posted on Facebook December 27, 2015

Father God, thank you for this new, blessed day of victory that You have made. Thank you for the gift of Your Son Jesus. Thank you for grace and mercy. Thank you for forgiveness. Great is Your faithfulness.

Save, heal, comfort, protect, deliver, encourage, strengthen, restore, provide for those in need right now. Thank you, Lord! In Jesus' name. Amen.

Posted on Facebook December 31, 2015

Dear Heavenly Father, thank you for bringing me through 2015. Thank you for keeping me and protecting me. Thank you for providing for me through change and transition.

As I look forward to the New Year, I pray to be and do all You have called me to be and do. I am in expectation for greater. I pray for wisdom, insight, and discernment. I pray for discipline and determination to reach my destiny.

Thank you for my family members, friends, and all those I care about. I pray for safety and salvation for all my loved ones. I pray for health, healing, and wholeness. I pray for breakthrough, turnaround and sudden change. I pray for supernatural manifestation even now.

You are faithful, and I trust You. Demonstrate Your power in my life. Show Yourself strong on my behalf. Use me for Your glory. I plead the blood of Jesus over everyone connected to me and pray a hedge of protection. Thank you for mercy, grace, forgiveness and favor. In Jesus' name. Amen! Happy Blessed 2016 all!

2016

Text to Family January 1, 2016

Father God, thank you for this 1st day of a new year that You have made. As for me and my family, we shall serve the Lord! I declare peace, provision, prosperity, protection and promotion over our lives. Thank you for change, transformation and restoration. Save, heal, deliver and set free. Thank you, Lord! In Jesus' name. Amen.

Posted on Facebook January 3, 2016

Father God, thank you for this new, blessed day of victory that You have made. I rejoice and am glad. Thank you for this new year of transformation. You are faithful and I trust You. Order my steps... Use me for Your glory... Demonstrate Your power in and through me... Show Yourself strong on my behalf.

I lift up family members, friends and acquaintances and pray for needs to be met. Save, heal, restore, comfort, redirect, deliver, strengthen, protect, provide for, and promote. God, You are faithful.

I lift up the Body of Christ and pray for boldness to declare Your Word. I pray for revival in our churches. I pray for holiness and righteousness to be the standard for our lives. I pray for our churches to be the extension of You providing hope, healing and love.

Holy Spirit, saturate our homes and churches with Your presence. We surrender to You. Save souls, heal hearts and change lives this day. We are ready to receive all You are sending. Thank you, Lord! In Jesus' mighty name. Amen.

Posted on Facebook January 6, 2016

Father God, I lift up the Woven ladies of Living Praise Christian Center and everyone who will attend our January Just Us Girls service on Sunday.

I thank You for Pastor Linda and am in expectation of a rich impartation. Holy Spirit, pour into her and let us receive everything You have for us. Bless every ministry gift, every worker and every attendee. I come against distractions that would try to hinder Your will being done. Touch bodies, heal hearts, restore relationships, revive dreams, renew passion. May we be all You created us to be. Thank you, Lord. In Jesus' name. Amen!

Posted on Facebook January 10, 2016

Father God, thank you for the powerful impartation received tonight from our very own Pastor and President Linda Hodge. Restore, refresh and rest her this week. Bless every ministry gift that came forth. We have been encouraged, empowered and armed with assignments to fulfill destiny. I pray for clarity where there is confusion. I pray for boldness where there is low self-esteem. I pray for confidence where there is insecurity. Your purpose and plan for our lives will be realized for we are women of destiny. I come against fear, doubt and unbelief. I come against distractions, delays and demonic detours. We are victorious. We walk by faith and favor surrounds us. Thank you, Lord for this year of transformation. We are moving forward. In Jesus' name, amen.

Text to Family January 14, 2016

Father God, I decree and declare peace and order to every household and come against confusion and frustration. Thank you, Lord. In Jesus' name. Amen.

Text to Family January 17, 2016

Father God, thank you for Your faithfulness in our lives. Order our steps. Lead and guide. Cover and protect. You can be trusted. Thank you! In Jesus' name, amen.

Text to Family January 29, 2016

Father God, thank you for this blessed day of victory. I declare peace over our lives and come against frustration, confusion and irritation. Heal, save, restore. Thank you, Lord! In Jesus' name. Amen.

Posted on Facebook February 4, 2016

Father God, thank you for this new, blessed day of victory that You have made. Thank you for new grace and mercy. Thank you for another opportunity to make a difference in the lives of others. Thank you for going before me to make the crooked places straight and giving Your angels charge over me. I plead the blood of Jesus over every mode of transportation I will take, in every city and state and on every road or highway I will travel as well as my family and friends. I will keep my mind stayed on You and You will keep me in perfect peace. Demonstrate Your power, Lord. I come against confusion, frustration, irritation and all demonic attacks. Thank you for protection from accident and injury. Thank you for healing and wholeness. Be glorified in and through my life. I honor and praise You Father. Thank you for wisdom, insight and discernment. Thank you for favor and good success. In Jesus' name. Amen. Have a blessed day and make wise choices.

Text to Family February 14, 2016

Father God, thank you for covering my family. Thank you for protecting each one. Thank you for healing and wholeness. Minister to each need. In Jesus' name. Amen.

Text to Family February 19, 2016

Father God, thank you for this new day. We are breathing so we are blessed. I claim victory this day. I plead the blood of Jesus over my family and believe You for healing and wholeness. Protect and guide this day. Strengthen and support. Thank you, Lord! In Jesus' name. Amen.

Text to Family February 20, 2016

Father God, thank you for the blessed day of victory You have made. Cover and protect us and help us to be who You have called us to be. Thank you for breakthrough, healing and wholeness. As for me and my family, we shall serve You Lord. Demonstrate Your power in our lives. We give You praise, honor and glory. In Jesus' name, Amen.

Posted on Facebook February 22, 2016

Father God, thank you for this new, already blessed day of victory that You have made. Thank you for waking me before the alarm. Thank you for change and transformation. Thank you for peace and order. Thank you for protection and provision. Thank you for forgiveness and favor. Thank you for salvation and security. Thank you for increase and overflow. Thank you for grace and mercy. Thank you for never leaving or forsaking me. Thank you for being my Refuge and Strong Tower. Thank you for assigning and equipping me. Thank you for healing and wholeness. Thank you for miracles, signs and wonders. Thank you for supernatural manifestation. Thank you for preservation and prosperity.

Father God, thank you for family and friends and everyone reading this post/praying this prayer. There is no one greater than You. I pray You minister to hearts, minds and needs right now. Deliver from drug, alcohol, nicotine and every other addiction. Deliver from darkness and demonic incarceration. Deliver from depression and discouragement. Heal physical, emotional, relational and mental pains and challenges.

Comfort, strengthen and encourage those going through a loss of a life or relationship. Provide financially for those in need. Secure shelter for those without a home. Bring order and peace where there is confusion and torment.

You are great and greatly to be praised. You are mighty and matchless in all Your ways. You are faithful and can be trusted. I bless Your name. Be glorified this day. Demonstrate Your power this day. Show Yourself strong this day. Shift atmospheres and environments this day. Use us for Your glory this day. Protect us and our family members from accident, injury and acts of violence. I give you all praise, glory and honor. In Jesus' mighty name. Amen.

Have a dynamic day and wonderful week!

Text to Family February 25, 2016

Father God, thank you for Your faithfulness to my family. I claim family salvation, family health and family favor. I plead the blood of Jesus over each member. Deliver and set free. Restore and make whole. Rest and refresh. Be glorified in my life. Thank you, Lord for the victory. In Jesus' mighty and matchless name. Amen.

Father God, the Living Praise Christian Center family lift up Elder John, Pastor Laura and their entire family as they celebrate the life of his dad Bill. Comfort them and encourage them during this time of loss and in the coming weeks and months as they get used to a new normal. Heal hearts, minds and bodies. You are faithful. You promise never to leave or forsake them. Minister to each one gathered and to those who couldn't attend and saturate them all with Your perfect peace. Thank you, Lord. In Jesus' mighty name. Amen.

We love you and we're here for you John Sibley and Laura Sibley!

Father God, You are not the author of confusion. I lift You up above every situation and circumstance. I bind every demonic force coming against our purpose and destiny. I come against frustration, irritation, deception. I plead the blood of Jesus over our lives. I declare peace, healing, prosperity, protection and victory. Chains are broken now. Thank you Father. In Jesus' mighty name. Amen.

Father God thank you for this blessed day of victory You have made. I pray for physical, mental and emotional health and strength. Heal and make whole. In Jesus' name.

Father God, thank you for our Pastors Dr. Fred Hodge and Linda Hodge! We are grateful for the vision You have assigned them and for the opportunity to serve in carrying it out. LPCC is transforming. Thank you for activation and elevation during these 6 SOS sessions and the rich impartation that went forth. We are in expectation that this will be our best year yet, collectively and individually. We walk in unity and excellence. We walk in honesty and integrity. We walk in the authority and power of Holy Spirit. We come against backlash, distractions and deception and plead the blood of Jesus over everyone connected to LPCC. Our eyes are open to see You and our ears are open to hear You. Use us for Your glory. Demonstrate Your power in and through us with signs following. We are a lighthouse in our community and win souls for Your kingdom. Rest and refresh us all tonight that we may be restored and ready for the week ahead. You are so faithful God. Thank you, Lord! In Jesus' mighty name. Hallelujah and Amen!

Text to Family March 7, 2016

Father God, thank you for this blessed day of victory. Cover and protect our going out and coming in. I come against backlash and all demonic attack. I plead the blood of Jesus over our lives and thank you for a hedge around us. Thank you for satisfying us with long life and showing us Your salvation. Demonstrate Your power. Thank you, Lord. In Jesus' name. Amen.

Text to Family March 8, 2016

Dear Heavenly Father, thank you for another blessed day of victory. I decree and declare peace, protection and order over our lives. Breakthrough, healing and restoration come now. I pray for salvation, repentance, rededication and deliverance. I plead the blood of Jesus over everyone connected to me. Thank you, Lord! You are faithful! In Jesus' mighty name. Hallelujah and Amen.

Posted on Facebook March 10, 2016

Good morning Abba! Thank you for giving me another chance to say thank you! I am grateful for and glad about this new, blessed day of victory You have made. Holy Spirit, I welcome Your guidance. Thank you, Lord! Praise You God! Hallelujah! Glory! In Jesus' name. Amen

Text to Family March 11, 2016

Father God, thank you for this new day of victory that You have made with new grace and mercy. We resist the enemy and submit to You Lord. I declare peace and good success over our day. I pray for change from the inside out. I pray our attitudes and actions are pleasing to You. Help us to make the right choice. I pray for protection as we go and come. Surround our schools and community and cover Jennifer and Maya. You are faithful, and I trust You. In Jesus' name. Amen. Love you all!

Posted on Facebook March 19, 2016

Father God, thank you for another year of life. I am grateful. I am excited and in expectation for this to be my best year yet. I am thankful for my family and friends and my pastors and church family (past and present). Happy Birthday to me! Be glorified in and through my life Lord! In Jesus' name. Amen.

Text to Family March 22, 2016

Father God, thank you for this blessed day of victory. Thank you for change and transformation. I call every family member saved, healed and whole. In Jesus' name...

Posted on Facebook March 29, 2016

Father God, thank you for anew day and new opportunity. Thank you for mercy, grace and forgiveness. Guide me this day. Cover my family members, church family and Facebook friends. Save, heal, comfort, encourage, deliver, protect and provide for. Thank you, Lord! In Jesus' name. Amen.

Text to Family April 12, 2016

Father God, thank you for this day. I declare victory over our lives. You are still on the throne. I plead the blood of Jesus over my family. We submit to You, resist the devil and he must flee. Minister strength, healing and wholeness. I trust You. Saturate our surroundings with Your Spirit. Thank you, Lord. In Jesus' name, Amen.

Text to Family April 12, 2016

Father God, I come against stress, worry, anxiety, fear, unbelief, discouragement and despair. I speak peace, health and wholeness. Thank you, Lord! In Jesus' name...

Text to Family April 16, 2016

Father God, thank you for this blessed day. Thank you for new mercies. Great is Your faithfulness. Forgive me of my sins. Help me to be more like You. I pray for peace in our home. Protect us as we go out and come in. I plead the blood of Jesus over every family member. Order our steps. Help us the walk in love one to another and communicate better. May we each submit to and serve You. I trust You. Thank you, Lord! In Jesus' name, Amen. Love you all

Text to Family April 25, 2016

Father God, thank you for another day. I pray we trust in You, seek You first and shine Your light. Heal, restore and make whole. Protect and provide. Thank you, Lord. In Jesus' name. Amen.

Text to Family May 11, 2016

Father God thank you for this new day of victory w/new grace and mercy. We trust You and cast every care upon You. Protect and cover. Thank you, Lord! In Jesus' name...

Text to Family May 15, 2016

Father God, we bless Your name and give You all the praise, glory and honor this day. I declare victory, healing, wholeness, protection and promotion over our lives. Thank you, Lord! In Jesus' name. Amen. Love each one of you!

Posted on Facebook May 15, 2016

Father God, thank you for the amazing leadership You have given us at LPCC in Dr. Fred Hodge and Pastor Linda Hodge! We are grateful for their commitment to You and their submission to the flow of the Holy Spirit. We are blessed by their passion for the people. We are thankful for their gifts, talents and abilities. Use us to support and sow into the vision. Overflow in their lives and exceed their expectations. Thank you, Lord for our year of transformation and season of supernatural manifestation. We give You all praise, honor and glory. In Jesus' mighty name. Amen

Father God, thank you for this new and blessed day of victory that You have made. I will rejoice and be glad in it. I come right now praying for a shift in the Baltimore forecast and weather. I pray for the rain to be held back on Saturday. When I marched into Hughes Stadium 25 years ago we had showers of blessings then the sprinkles stopped and the sun came out. I am praying for a bright sunny Saturday so that all graduates, family members and friends who attend can sit outside in Hughes Stadium together to celebrate our loved ones. Hold back the rain Lord.

I also pray for safe travels for everyone going and coming not just for this Commencement but all across the country. I pray for peace, protection and favor. I come against accident, injury and incidents. I come against delays, distractions and demonic interference. I come against breakdowns and equipment malfunction and failure. I come against stress, worry, anxiety and confusion. Order our steps. Design our day. You are faithful!

I lift up those in/facing a challenging situation. Heal, save, deliver, comfort, encourage, strengthen and provide. Meet every need. Manifest the miraculous. Thank you, Lord! In Jesus' name. Amen.

Father God, thank you for Your continued hand of protection over my life and over the lives of my family members and loved ones. I plead the blood of Jesus over everyone connected to me. Cover and surround. Intervene right now. Rest us tonight.

Father, I lift up the campus and graduation of Morgan State University and pray for Your Presence to saturate the environment and atmosphere. I pray for peace and cooperation. I pray for order and adherence to direction. I pray for unity and for hearts and minds to be on one accord. I come against confusion, frustration, accident, injury and all demonic activity. Demonstrate Your power Lord.

I pray it's a glorious day celebrating success. I pray for supernatural physical and mental strength for everyone. Thank you, Lord! You are faithful. In Jesus' mighty name. Amen.

Text to Family May 25, 2016

Father God thank you for this new, blessed day of victory that You have made. Heal, save, protect, deliver, change and transform. Thank you, Lord. In Jesus' name...

Posted on Facebook May 29, 2016

Father God, thank you for this new, blessed day of victory that You have made. Thank you for new grace and mercy this day. Great is Your faithfulness. Your compassion fail not. Thank you for safety and security in salvation. Thank you for the shed blood of Your Son Jesus that through receiving Him as Savior and Lord we may have eternal life. Forgive me of my sins and cleanse me from all unrighteousness. Create in me a clean heart and renew a right spirit within me. Holy Spirit, guide. There is no one greater than You God. I trust in You. I seek You first. I surrender to You. Minister to the needs of my family members, friends, loved ones and anyone praying this prayer. Save, heal, comfort, strengthen, encourage, deliver, provide for, protect, promote. Thank you, Lord! In Jesus' mighty name. Amen.

Text to Family June 1, 2016

Father God, thank you for this new day. You are faithful and I trust You. Cover and protect. Save, heal and deliver. I come against delays, disobedience, deception and demonic activities. Demonstrate Your power. Thank you, Lord! In Jesus' name. Amen. Love you family. Going back to bed now. ☺

Text to Family June 8, 2016

Father God, thank you for this new day. Cover and protect my family. Minister to every need. Thank you, Lord. In Jesus' name. Amen

Posted on Facebook June 8, 2016

Father God, thank you for this new and blessed day and season of victory. Thank you for the wake up call. Thank you for Your covering and protection. Thank you for mercy and grace. Thank you for forgiving and favoring me. No weapon formed against me, my family, my loved ones, my church family, my community, my friends or anyone connected to me shall prosper.

I pray for salvation decisions this day. I pray for rededications this day. I lift up to You the hurting, the lost, the offended, the deceived, the depressed, the discouraged, the oppressed, the abused, the addicted, the bound. Reveal and uncover. Heal and deliver Lord.

I plead the blood of Jesus over our homes, neighborhoods, communities, schools, college campuses, churches, parks, workplaces, and wherever people gather. Cover airports and harbors and train and bus stations. Cover freeways and highways.

I come against mass destruction and demonic activity and interference. I pray for the church of the Living God to wake up and stand up. I pray for deliverance and breakthrough. I pray for turnaround and sudden change. Heal hearts, minds, hurts and emotions. Restore relationships and marriages.

I come against generational curses, open doors and enemy encroachment. I come against frustration, confusion and lies from the enemy. Father, You are faithful. I pray for revival in this land.

Thank you, Lord for protection. Thank you for wisdom, insight and discernment. Thank you for direction. Thank you for gracing, anointing and equipping. Thank you for already giving us the victory. We stand still to see Your salvation and fulfill Your purpose. Demonstrate Your power.

Thank you, Lord! There is no one greater than You Father. There is none like You. No one can compare to You. You are worthy of all praise, glory and honor. Be glorified in and through our lives. I'm looking for the miraculous and expect the impossible. Do what only You can do. Thank you for transformation.

In the mighty and matchless name of Jesus I pray with thanksgiving. Amen. Hallelujah! Glory to God!

Text to Family June 19, 2016

Father God, I thank you for the victory that is ours in Christ Jesus. Cover us this day. Protect our going out and coming in. Heal and deliver. In Jesus' name. Amen.

Posted on Facebook June 27, 2016

Father God, thank you for this new, super early day of victory that You have made. I will rejoice and be glad in it. Thank you for safe travels as I prepare to drive to BWI on just 2 hours of sleep. Thank you for turbulent-free, favor-filled travel from here to CA. Orchestrate our day. Use me for Your glory. Thank you for a power-packed 12 days of learning, family fun and fellowship with friends. I look forward to what the future holds. Guide my steps. Bless, cover and protect my family and friends. Thank you, Lord! In Jesus' name. Amen.

Posted on Facebook July 1, 2016

Singing: It's a new season, it's a new day. A fresh anointing is flowing my way. It's a season of power and prosperity. It's a new season coming to me.

Hello July 1st! Father God, thank you for this new day and month of victory that You have made. Order my steps. Orchestrate my plans. Open doors. Demonstrate Your power and be glorified in and through my life. Thank you, Lord! You are faithful, and I am grateful. Thank you, Lord for forgiving me and favoring me. Thank you for protection and provision. Thank you for surrounding me with peace. Thank you for wisdom, understanding, discernment and insight. Thank you for increase and overflow. Bless my family and friends. I give You all praise, honor and glory. In Jesus' mighty name. Amen. Have a safe holiday weekend!

Posted on Facebook July 6, 2016

Father God, I humble myself seeking Your face and praying on behalf of this country. Forgive me of my sins. Create in me a clean heart and renew a right spirit continually.

I lift up the Sterling and Castile families to You and the family, friends and communities of all others who have been so senselessly killed. Comfort and heal and provide for their needs. Minister peace like only You can during this trying time.

I pray for justice to prevail. I come against hate, arrogance and pride, in Jesus' name. Reveal and remove those killing and those allowing the killing to continue without consequence. I pray for justice.

I pray for a return to righteousness. I pray for honesty and integrity to govern our lives. I pray for Your people to humble themselves, pray, seek Your face and turn from their wicked ways. You promise to hear from heaven, forgive our sins and heal our land. Our land needs healing.

Father God, I plead the blood of Jesus over our neighborhoods and come against bloodshed. I come against demonic influence and activity. Protect and cover our loved ones. I come against premature, untimely death. Lord, help.

Saturate our country with peace. I pray for wise, godly counsel for those in authority. .... Thank you, Lord. In Jesus' name. Amen.

Text to Family July 7, 2016

Father God, thank you for this blessed day of victory You have made. I plead the blood of Jesus over every loved one from the crown of our head to the soles of our feet and pray for protection. I come against all demonic activity and interference. I come against premature death and declare we shall fulfill Your purpose for our lives. Thank you, Lord. In Jesus' name. Amen

Text to Family July 8, 2016

Father God, thank you for this day of victory You have made. You have not given us a spirit of fear but of power, love and a sound well-balanced mind. May we walk in Your power, love and strength. Give us wisdom and discernment. May we seek to please You. Thank you for covering, protecting and directing. In Jesus' name. Amen

Text to Family July 10, 2016

Singing... Holy Spirit, You are welcome here. Come flood this place and fill the atmosphere.....Your glory, God is what our hearts long for. To be overcome by Your presence, Lord. Your presence, Lord. Have an amazing day! Look for and expect God's glory.

Posted on Facebook July 12, 2016

Father God, thank you.... This is the day that the Lord has made. I will rejoice. I will rejoice. I will rejoice and be glad and grateful in it. Are you breathing? Praise the Lord! Hallelujah! Glory to God!

Text to Family July 22, 2016

Father God, thank you for this blessed day of victory and favor. I declare peace, protection and provision over our lives. I come against confusion, frustration, depression and discouragement. I pray for salvation, rededication, healing and deliverance. Order our steps. Demonstrate Your power. Thank you, Lord. In Jesus' name.

Posted on Facebook July 24, 2016, 9:16 am

Dear Heavenly Father, thank you for this blessed day of victory that You have made. I will rejoice and be glad. You are worthy to be praised. There is no one greater than You. There is no force stronger than You. Great is Your faithfulness. Thank you for new mercy and fresh grace. Thank you for Your love and forgiveness. Thank you for never leaving or forsaking us. Create in me a clean heart and renew a right spirit within me. Forgive me of my sins and may my attitude and actions be pleasing to You. Hallelujah! Praise you God. I bless Your name. Thank you Father. Holy Spirit, minister.

Right now, I lift up everyone angry at You. I lift up everyone who has been hurt by those who were to care for and protect them. I lift up everyone who has been offended by a word, a look or an action committed by those who are called to lead and guide them, teach or encourage. I lift up everyone who feel separated from You. I lift up everyone discouraged, depressed or beaten down by life. I lift up everyone deceived by the enemy. I lift up everyone currently serving and submitted to Satan. Have mercy Lord. Heal Lord. Save Lord. Deliver Lord. You wish that none perish.

I plead the blood of Jesus over each one right now. I pray for salvation to come to them now. I pray for healing in their heart and mind. I pray for deliverance from bondage and addiction. I pray for the one who won't forgive themselves. I pray for renewal, repentance and refreshment.

I pray for rededication and submission to You. Penetrate the dark places. Shine Your light. Bring peace.

I come against pride. I come against deception. I come against demonic attack and interference. I come against destructive behavior. Demonstrate Your power. Send a word or a hug. Reconcile family members. Restore households. Thank you for turnaround and break-through. Thank you for healing and wholeness. Thank you for change and transformation. You are faithful and can be trusted. Thank you for hearing and answering. In the mighty and matchless name of Jesus I pray. Amen.

Posted on Facebook July 24, 2016

Father God, we pray for 100% containment of the fires in Santa Clarita. We speak peace to the winds. We pray for rain in Southern California. We pray for supernatural intervention. We pray for mental, emotional and physical strength of the firefighters and everyone impacted. Demonstrate Your power Lord. We give You all glory, honor and praise. In Jesus' name. Amen.

Text to Family August 5, 2016

Good morning family! This is the day that the Lord has made rejoice and be glad. You are victorious in Christ Jesus! Glory to God! Have an amazing day and weekend!

Text to Family August 14, 2016

Father God, thank you for another blessed day of victory. Minister to every heart and mind. Demonstrate Your power through us. In Jesus' name. Amen. Love you, fam!

Posted on Facebook August 16, 2016

Father God, thank you for this new day of victory that You have made. I rejoice and am glad. You are faithful, and I trust You. Thank you for new mercy and grace. Thank you for forgiveness and favor. Thank you for protection and provision.

I declare peace over this day in our homes, on our streets and in our schools. Surround every school campus and saturate every classroom.

May parents be calm, teachers and staff pleasant and students prepared to learn.

I pray for safety in our travels and come against anxiety, stress and road rage. I pray for wisdom and direction. On one of the hottest days of the year may everyone work together for the good of all. Let there be a supernatural cooling.

Demonstrate Your power in and through our lives this day. I pray every school is an excellent environment for learning. I plead the blood of Jesus over our schools and come against violence and destruction. I pray for a continual hedge of protection. Satan, you cannot have our children, our families.

Thank you, Lord for good success. Thank you, Lord for cooperation. Thank you, Lord for resources. Thank you, Lord for every need met. I give you the praise, honor and glory! In the mighty and matchless name of Jesus. Amen.

Posted on Facebook August 23, 2016

Come against fear, anxiety, worry and stress, in Jesus' name. Stay in faith and maintain a healthy mind, body and environment through the Word and worship. God, You're faithful!

Text to Family August 25, 2016

Father God, You are faithful and I trust You. You are bigger than any situation now or to come. Cover my family. Heal, deliver and set free. I come against stress, worry, fear and anxiety. Demonstrate Your power. Thank you, Lord for breakthrough and turnaround. We are victorious. In Jesus' mighty and matchless name. Amen.

Text to Family September 12, 2016

Father God, thank you for this blessed week of victory. I declare health, healing, wholeness and soundness in our mind, body, emotions, relationships and finances. Deliver and set free. Demonstrate Your power. Thank you, Lord. In Jesus' mighty name. Amen. God is faithful. Just believe.

Text to Hubby September 19, 2016

Father God, I pray for peace of mind and calm to Robert's organs and functions. I pray for favor and kindness from all supervisors and coworkers. Thank you, Lord for a blessed victorious day and week. In Jesus' name. Amen.

Text to Family September 21, 2016

Father God, I plead the blood of Jesus over every family member and loved one and thank you for Your protection. No one connected to me shall be lost or come to premature death. I come against fear, discouragement, depression and confusion in Jesus' name. Saturate all hearts and minds with Your love, peace and joy. In Jesus' mighty name, Amen. Trust God!

Posted on Facebook September 30, 2016

Father God, You know all things and what will occur before it happens. I pray for safety and no loss of life or property in the event of an earthquake. I pray for reduced stress on the San Andreas fault and the San Jacinto fault system. I pray for wisdom and preparedness. Thank you, Lord for Your hand of protection. We are poised and prayerful. You are faithful. In Jesus' name. Amen.

Posted on Facebook October 2, 2016

Father God, I pray for wisdom in how to vote in all areas and for women and men of integrity to rise to leadership. I still trust You and my hope is in You. In Jesus' name. Amen.

Posted on Facebook October 3, 2016

Father God, thank you for a new beginning. Thank you for the opportunity to reflect and repent not just today but every day. I pray for forgiveness of sins. I pray for a year of good health, happiness, prosperity and peace. I pray for a year of pursuing purpose and Your perfect will for our lives. I pray for deliverance and restoration and surrender and submission to Your Word. Demonstrate Your power in the lives of Your people. I pray that those called by Your name would humble ourselves, pray, seek Your face and turn from our wicked ways. You then promise to hear from heaven, forgive our sins and heal our land. You are faithful. Thank you, Lord. I give You all the praise, glory and honor. In Jesus' mighty name , I pray. Amen.

Text to Hubby October 3, 2016

Father God, thank you for this blessed day of victory that You have made. We rejoice and we are glad. I pray Your perfect will be done concerning Robert and Blue Shield. I pray for favor and open doors. Holy Spirit, guide and direct. Strengthen and encourage. You are faithful and we trust You. Minister to Robert this day. Thank you, Lord. In Jesus' name. Amen. Love you Babe!

Posted on Facebook October 5, 2016

Father God, I come against the foolery, ignorance, scare tactics, pranks, copycats, clowning and all demonic activity and influence in the name of Jesus. Amen

Posted on Facebook October 6, 2016

Father God ,we speak peace to the winds and waves of Hurricane Matthew and pray a hedge of protection over the areas expecting to be impacted in Florida, Georgia and the Carolinas over the next few days. Cover people and property. We pray for recovery and restoration of services for the areas already hit. Demonstrate Your power God. Thank you, Lord. In Jesus' name. Amen.

Posted on Facebook October 14, 2016

And at midnight Tisha prayed and sang praises unto God....You are my strength, strength like no other. Father God, thank you for being my Protector and Covering. Thank you for the shift that has taken place. Thank you for clarity and understanding. Thank you for insight and revelation. Thank you for promotion, increase and overflow. Thank you for being my Light and my Deliverer. I fear no man. You are faithful. I stand still to see Your plans unfold in my life. My future is written, sealed and copyrighted. In Jesus' mighty name. Amen.

Posted on Facebook October 20, 2016

Father God, I pray for safe travels going and coming for everyone making their way to the family reunion. Morgan is family. It's been 25 years since finishing undergrad and I am thankful. Morgan gave me roots to grow and wings to soar both as a student and staff member. I am grateful. Thank you for the friendships that continue even today. As we reconnect with some we may not have seen since 911 or remember those who are no longer with us, may this be our best Homecoming yet. Thank you for protection and provision. In Jesus' name. Amen!

Text to Family October 23, 2016

Father God, thank you for this blessed day that You have made. Thank you for Your continued faithfulness in our lives. Minister to each need this week. In Jesus' name. Amen.

Text to Hubby October 25, 2016

Father God, thank you for this blessed day that You have made. We rejoice and am glad. Thank you for Your constant care over us. Guide us Holy Spirit. Protect our family and loved ones. I plead the blood of Jesus over everyone connected to me. Bless Robert this day and exceed his expectations. Thank you, Lord. In Jesus name. Amen. Love you Babe!

Text to Family November 9, 2016

Family! This is the day that the Lord has made. Rejoice and be glad. No matter who is president, God is King. He is in control and my confidence and trust is in Him.

Text to Family November 9, 2016

Father God, thank you for never leaving or forsaking us. Thank you for strength for every assignment. You are faithful. I will continue to trust You. Grateful!

Posted on Facebook November 17, 2016, 9:00 am

Father God, thank you for the blessing and gift You placed in my life 11 years ago when I joined LPCC March 16, 2005. I lift up Pastor Linda

Hodge and pray You continue to cover, empower and strengthen her to fulfill all You have for her to accomplish. Thank you for her example as a woman, wife, mother, teacher, preacher and mentor. Overflow in her life in this season. I praise God for my Pastors. In Jesus' name. Amen.

Posted on Facebook November 22, 2016, 5:20 pm

Father God, I thank you our dynamic Pastors Dr. Fred and Linda Hodge and the vision You have given them for the LPCC family and the world. It shall speak. Continue to minister to and through them. I lift up Bishop Murphy, his family and congregation and pray for safe travels and protection. I pray hearts and minds would be ready to participate in this night of worship and receive all You have in store. I pray everyone on post are submitted to the Holy Spirit. I am in expectation of miracles, signs and wonders. Save, heal, deliver and set free. Thank you, Lord! You are faithful. I give You all the glory, honor and praise. In Jesus' mighty name. Amen

Text to Hubby December 27, 2016

Father God, thank you for another blessed day of victory that You have made. Thank you for going before Robert this day to make every crooked place straight. Thank you for protection from accident and injury. Thank you for provision for every need. Thank you for peace that surround and saturate his presence. Thank you for health and healing in his body. I come against cold, cough and congestion. I pray for good success in this day and the remainder of this year. Demonstrate Your power Father. Thank you, Lord. In Jesus' mighty name, amen.

Posted on Facebook December 30, 2016

Father God, thank you for another blessed day of victory! You made this day and I am grateful and glad. I rejoice in Your faithfulness. I celebrate because I am forgiven. There is no one greater than You. Thank you for brand new mercies. Your compassions fail not. Thank you for new grace this day!

Father God, for many 2016 has been a challenging year. I lift up my family, friends, classmates, acquaintances, colleagues and everyone reading this post. Minister to each need. You understand if no one else does. You care more than anyone can. You are able to help better than anyone.

You see that one experiencing a health concern. I pray for mental and emotional strength to go through the physical challenge. I pray for accuracy in diagnosis and treatment. I pray for the best medical, caring team. I pray for the miraculous to manifest. I pray for grace for the family members and caregivers.

You see the one experiencing the loss of a loved one. Heal the hurt, the pain, the grief. Minister peace when emotions are out of control. Minister hope when there seems to be no way life can go one without that loved one. Minister joy where depression and discouragement may try to take up residence. Wrap them in Your love. Rest them in Your presence. Meet the needs where there is now a void.

Father God, provide for those in need of shelter, food, clothes. Restore fractured and damaged relationships. Deliver and set free from addiction and demonic influence. Open doors for employment, opportunities and business resources. Provide for educational expenses. Strengthen those just weary from life.

I pray for salvation for those who don't know You. I pray for rededication for those who walked away from You. I pray for forgiveness to be given and received so life can be lived to the fullest. Heal Lord.

Thank you for lessons learned in 2016 and for never leaving me or forsaking me. As I prepare for 2017 I am excited for greater. I am excited to fulfill purpose. I am excited for increase, promotion and elevation. I am excited for new things. I am excited for growth. I am excited to experience the plans You have for me. I am excited for manifestation and overflow.

Cover everyone I love and care for. Protect from dangers seen and unseen. Save from accident and injury. I plead the blood of Jesus and come against untimely, premature death. We shall live to declare the mighty works of the Lord. You are faithful. I trust You. In the mighty, matchless, majestic name of Jesus I pray with Thanksgiving. Amen!

Happy Blessed New Year!

About the Author

Tisha Lynton Rose was born in the Caribbean on the beautiful island of St. Thomas, USVI to wonderful parents, John and Joan Lynton. Upon graduation from high school, she went to college at Morgan State University in Baltimore, Maryland where she earned a Bachelor's of Science Degree in Management. While matriculating at Morgan State, Tisha was active in many organizations which included a year with the world-renown Morgan State University choir and three years in Student Government Association. She served as president of her senior class and earned a Masters of Business Administration while working at Morgan full-time.

Before moving to Southern California, she served as the first church Administrator & Assistant to the pastor at Huber Memorial Church in Baltimore, Maryland. She moved to California to work as Program Manager for Honda Campus All-Star Challenge (HCASC), an educational program for America's historically black colleges and universities (HBCUs). In addition to her full-time job, she served as the Partners Ministry Team Director and a WOVEN Women's Ministry cabinet member along with volunteering with other organizations.

Tisha completed Living Praise Christian Institute 3-year program finishing as the Valedictorian. She in no way leads a boring life. She desires to impact the lives of others in schools and the community by helping them reach their goals. Tisha would like to restore hope to those who are hopeless and gets joy in helping others.

She launched her event planning business, TRose Productions in the Spring of 2017 after planning events for the last 20 years.

Tisha is married to her loving, caring and supportive husband Robert for seven years and have two daughters. Jennifer is a freshman at Morgan State University and Maya is a freshman in high school. The family recently relocated to Arizona.